From AI-Support to AI-First Enterprises

Artificial intelligence (AI) is becoming an increasingly visible element of business management, influencing not only operational processes but also strategic planning, financial management, leadership, and organisational governance. This book examines these changes from an interdisciplinary perspective, combining management studies, innovation research, AI ethics, and enterprise decision-making. Rather than presenting artificial intelligence solely as a technological tool, the volume explores its growing role in shaping organisational structures, managerial practices, and new models of leadership.

The chapters discuss integrated AI systems, intelligent process automation, predictive analytics, and AI-supported decision-making across strategic, operational, and financial dimensions. Particular attention is devoted to the appearance of humanoid and virtual leaders, including the cases of Mika, the humanoid CEO, and Tang Yu, the virtual CEO. These examples are used to analyse how AI is increasingly embedded within executive and managerial functions, raising important questions about accountability, transparency, human oversight, explainability, and the future role of managers in organisations.

The volume additionally includes an empirical market analysis conducted among 192 enterprises representing sectors such as manufacturing, logistics, finance, trade, technology, and services. The findings illustrate how organisations implement AI technologies, what barriers they encounter, and how intelligent systems influence organisational efficiency, strategic adaptability, customer relations, and innovation processes.

At the same time, the book addresses broader organisational and societal implications connected with AI adoption, including workforce transformation, algorithmic bias, governance challenges, and changing forms of human–machine collaboration. Combining theoretical discussion with case studies and practical examples, the volume offers a critical and accessible examination of how artificial intelligence is influencing entrepreneurship, enterprise management, and leadership in the digital economy.

From AI-Support to AI-First Enterprises

Transformation of Entrepreneurship, Management, and Leadership

Ida Skubis, Judyta Kabus, Jolanta Wodarska, Krzysztof Wodarski, and Klaudia Grębowiec

CRC Press
Taylor & Francis Group
Boca Raton London New York

CRC Press is an imprint of the
Taylor & Francis Group, an **informa** business

First edition published 2027
by CRC Press
2385 NW Executive Center Drive, Suite 320, Boca Raton FL 33431

and by CRC Press
4 Park Square, Milton Park, Abingdon, Oxon, OX14 4RN

CRC Press is an imprint of Taylor & Francis Group, LLC

ISBN: 9781041407003 (hbk)
ISBN: 9781041407010 (pbk)
ISBN: 9781042024131 (ebk)

DOI: 10.1201/9781042024131

Typeset in Times
by Newgen Publishing UK

Contents

Authors

Ida Skubis, Silesian University of Technology.

Judyta Kabus, Jan Dlugosz University in Czestochowa.

Jolanta Wodarska, Silesian University of Technology.

Krzysztof Wodarski, Silesian University of Technology.

Klaudia Grębowiec, Czestochowa University of Technology.

Introduction

Contemporary enterprises increasingly operate in environments where decision-making, coordination, and organisational adaptation depend on the continuous processing of large-scale data flows rather than solely on human interpretation and managerial intuition. In this context, artificial intelligence is no longer confined to the role of a technological instrument supporting isolated business functions. Instead, AI systems are becoming embedded within the structural logic of enterprises themselves, influencing how organisations forecast uncertainty, allocate resources, manage operations, evaluate performance, and formulate strategic priorities. The growing integration of predictive analytics, intelligent automation, machine learning, and generative systems reflects a broader organisational transition from digitally supported management towards AI-oriented enterprise architectures characterised by continuous data-driven adaptation and algorithmically mediated governance (Bharadwaj et al., 2013; Vial, 2019).

This transition emerges simultaneously with broader transformations affecting the global economy, labor structures, and competitive dynamics. Enterprises function in increasingly volatile and technologically intensive environments, where organisational survival and growth depend on the ability to respond rapidly to changing market conditions, customer expectations, regulatory requirements, and technological disruptions. Under these conditions, traditional decision-making models based primarily on periodic reporting, hierarchical communication, and limited analytical capacity are increasingly insufficient. Artificial intelligence expands the analytical and operational capabilities of organisations by enabling real time interpretation of complex datasets, predictive forecasting, adaptive learning, and automated optimisation of business processes (Wodarski et al., 2025; Warner & Wäger, 2019).

The integration of AI into enterprise environments also reflects a broader change in the understanding of digital transformation itself. Earlier phases of digitalisation were largely focused on implementing fragmented technological tools intended to improve efficiency within isolated organisational functions, such as accounting systems, enterprise resource planning platforms, or customer relationship management solutions. Contemporary AI-driven transformation differs fundamentally because it increasingly affects organisational logic,

DOI:10.1201/9781042024131-1

governance structures, and managerial processes rather than merely supporting existing activities. AI systems now participate in shaping decisions, coordinating operations, prioritizing strategic objectives, and structuring organisational interactions (Jöhnk et al., 2021).

The increasing integration of AI into enterprise environments is also connected to the broader development of intelligent communication infrastructures and digital interaction systems. Research on multilingual dialogue systems and AI-supported communication platforms demonstrates that conversational AI increasingly supports customer interaction, information exchange, and operational coordination in digitally transformed organisations (Wołk et al., 2022). Similarly, studies on multilingual chatbots in e-commerce environments indicate that AI-driven communication systems contribute to the automation and personalisation of enterprise-consumer interactions while simultaneously reshaping digital service models (Wołk et al., 2021).

Consequently, enterprises are gradually evolving from "AI-support" organisations towards "AI-first" organisations. In AI-support environments, artificial intelligence primarily functions as a decision-support mechanism that assists managers by providing analytics, forecasts, or automation of repetitive tasks. By contrast, AI-first enterprises embed algorithmic systems within the core structures of organisational coordination and governance. In such organisations, AI increasingly influences strategic planning, operational management, financial oversight, customer interactions, innovation processes, and even leadership structures. Artificial intelligence thus becomes not merely a technical infrastructure but an organisational actor shaping the dynamics of enterprise development.

This transformation is particularly visible in the domains of entrepreneurship, management, and leadership. AI systems support entrepreneurial activities by accelerating innovation cycles, identifying emerging market opportunities, facilitating experimentation, and enabling the development of new business models based on digital ecosystems and platform economies (Nambisan et al., 2019). AI-driven transformation also increasingly affects marketing strategies, consumer engagement, and digital branding practices. Comparative analyses of AI platforms used in marketing environments demonstrate that organisations rely on intelligent systems not only for automation and analytics but also for content generation, audience targeting, and strategic communication management (Skubis & Damas, 2025). These developments suggest that AI is becoming integrated into the symbolic and communicative dimensions of enterprise activity, influencing how organisations position themselves within competitive digital markets. Simultaneously, management processes are becoming increasingly data-driven, predictive, and adaptive. Integrated AI systems enable enterprises to connect strategic, operational, and financial layers of decision-making into coherent analytical environments capable of responding continuously to internal and external changes.

AI-driven transformation also intersects with broader discussions concerning innovation management and organisational adaptation within digitally transformed economies. Research on innovative business strategies in the era of digital transformation indicates that enterprises increasingly combine AI technologies with process innovation, strategic flexibility, and data-oriented organisational models to maintain competitiveness within rapidly evolving markets (Kabus et al., 2026). At the same time, the development of AI-oriented enterprises is closely linked to broader discussions concerning human–AI collaboration, organisational competencies, and managerial adaptation. Emerging studies on human–AI collaboration emphasise that future organisational models will likely depend not on replacing human actors, but on developing sustainable forms of cooperation between human expertise and AI-driven analytical systems (Skubis et al., 2026).

The transformation towards AI-oriented enterprises additionally requires the redefinition of managerial competencies and organisational roles. Research on process-project organisations highlights that contemporary managers increasingly need interdisciplinary capabilities combining strategic management, technological understanding, organisational coordination, and ethical oversight (Skubis & Bijańska, 2024). In digitally transformed organisational environments, managerial effectiveness depends not only on operational expertise but also on the ability to supervise complex socio-technical systems integrating human and algorithmic decision-making processes.

The development of AI-based organisational structures also contributes to the emergence of new forms of leadership and managerial authority. Traditional models of leadership have historically been associated with human judgment, interpersonal communication, emotional intelligence, and hierarchical supervision. However, the increasing use of AI systems in executive decision-making introduces algorithmic forms of coordination and governance that reshape organisational authority structures. AI-driven systems are increasingly involved in strategic analysis, operational prioritisation, performance evaluation, and resource allocation, thereby altering the relationship between human managers and technological systems within enterprises (Mikalef & Gupta, 2021).

At the same time, the growing organisational role of AI generates important ethical, social, and regulatory challenges. The implementation of AI systems raises questions regarding transparency, explainability, accountability, surveillance, bias, and human oversight. As enterprises delegate greater analytical and operational authority to algorithms, concerns emerge regarding the opacity of decision-making processes and the potential diffusion of responsibility. Algorithmic systems may reinforce existing inequalities, reproduce biased outcomes, or generate decisions that remain difficult to interpret and audit (Dwivedi et al., 2021). Consequently, responsible AI governance becomes a fundamental requirement for organisations seeking to integrate artificial intelligence sustainably and ethically into enterprise structures.

The growing organisational reliance on AI systems additionally intensifies discussions concerning trustworthy AI and responsible governance frameworks. Research on AI governance in healthcare environments demonstrates that transparency, explainability, and ethical supervision remain fundamental conditions for maintaining trust in AI-supported decision-making systems, particularly in contexts involving high-impact organisational and societal consequences (Skubis et al., 2025). These governance-related challenges increasingly extend beyond healthcare and affect enterprise management more broadly, especially as organisations integrate AI into strategic and operational structures.

The successful implementation of AI also depends on organisational readiness and institutional adaptation. Enterprises require not only technological infrastructure but also appropriate governance mechanisms, interdisciplinary competencies, and organisational cultures capable of supporting continuous learning and data-oriented decision-making. AI transformation therefore involves changes in managerial practices, employee roles, organisational communication, and strategic thinking. Managers increasingly operate in hybrid environments where human judgment interacts continuously with algorithmic recommendations and automated systems.

Against this background, the present book, *From AI-Support to AI-First Enterprises: Transformation of Entrepreneurship, Management, and Leadership*, examines how artificial intelligence is reshaping contemporary enterprises and redefining organisational governance. The volume explores the transition from fragmented AI applications towards integrated AI-driven organisational architectures. Particular attention is devoted to the transformation of entrepreneurship, strategic and operational management, financial systems, leadership structures, and decision-making processes under conditions of increasing algorithmic integration.

The book advances the argument that artificial intelligence should no longer be understood exclusively as a technological support mechanism. Instead, AI increasingly functions as a structural component of enterprise governance that shapes how organisations process information, coordinate activities, formulate strategies, and distribute responsibility. The transition towards AI-first enterprises therefore represents not merely technological modernisation but a deeper transformation in the logic of organisational functioning.

Importantly, the volume adopts a critical and interdisciplinary perspective on AI-driven enterprise transformation. While artificial intelligence offers substantial opportunities related to efficiency, innovation, scalability, and organisational adaptability, its implementation also requires careful reflection on governance, ethics, accountability, and human agency. The future of AI-driven enterprises will depend not only on advances in algorithms and automation but also on the capacity of organisations to establish transparent, human-centred, and responsible governance structures capable of balancing technological capability with ethical and organisational sustainability.

The chapters included in this volume collectively contribute to ongoing debates concerning the future of enterprises in the age of artificial intelligence. Through theoretical analyses and empirical case studies, the book examines how AI transforms entrepreneurship, management, and leadership, while simultaneously raising new questions regarding organisational control, strategic governance, and the evolving relationship between human and artificial decision-making systems.

REFERENCES

Bharadwaj, A., El Sawy, O. A., Pavlou, P. A., & Venkatraman, N. (2013). Digital business strategy: Toward a next generation of insights. *MIS Quarterly, 37*(2), 471–482. https://doi.org/10.25300/MISQ/2013/37:2.3

Dwivedi, Y. K., Hughes, L., Ismagilova, E., Aarts, G., Coombs, C., Crick, T., et al. (2021). Artificial Intelligence (AI): Multidisciplinary perspectives on emerging challenges, opportunities, and agenda for research, practice and policy. *International Journal of Information Management, 57*, 101994. https://doi.org/10.1016/j.ijinfomgt.2019.08.002

Jöhnk, J., Weißert, M., & Wyrtki, K. (2021). Ready or not, AI comes-An interview study of organizational AI readiness factors. *Business & Information Systems Engineering, 63*, 5–20. https://doi.org/10.1007/s12599-020-00676-7

Kabus, J., Antczak, J., Skubis, I., & Zajkowska, M. (2026). *Innovative business strategies: In the era of digital transformation*. Taylor & Francis.

Mikalef, P., & Gupta, M. (2021). Artificial intelligence capability: Conceptualization, measurement calibration, and empirical study on its impact on organizational creativity and firm performance. *Information & Management, 58*(3), 103434. https://doi.org/10.1016/j.im.2021.103434

Nambisan, S., Wright, M., & Feldman, M. (2019). The digital transformation of innovation and entrepreneurship: Progress, challenges and key themes. *Research Policy, 48*(8), 103773. https://doi.org/10.1016/j.respol.2019.03.018

Skubis, I., & Bijańska, J. (2024). The role and competencies of managers in contemporary process-project organizations. *Scientific Papers of Silesian University of Technology – Organization and Management Series, 198*, 399–510. https://managementpapers.polsl.pl/wp-content/uploads/2024/07/198-Skubis-Bijańska.pdf

Skubis, I., & Damas, K. (2025). Harnessing artificial intelligence in marketing: Comparative analysis of platforms and their features, capabilities, and applications. *Linguistic and Philosophical Investigations, 24*(1), 43–60.

Skubis, I., Wodarski, K., & Lütge, Ch. (2025). Ethical considerations, prompt management and linguistic challenges in ChatGPT's responses to controversial topics: A comparative analysis of GPT-3.5 and GPT-4.0 in the case study on sex robot influencers. *Review of Contemporary Philosophy*, *24*(1), 54–82.

Skubis, I., Xerri, D., & Adamovic, M. (2026). *Human–AI collaboration in research: Practical applications, ethical frameworks, and future directions* (1st ed.). CRC Press.

Vial, G. (2019). Understanding digital transformation: A review and a research agenda. *The Journal of Strategic Information Systems*, *28*(2), 118–144. https://doi.org/10.1016/j.jsis.2019.01.003

Warner, K. S. R., & Wäger, M. (2019). Building dynamic capabilities for digital transformation: An ongoing process of strategic renewal. *Long Range Planning, 52*(3), 326–349. https://doi.org/10.1016/j.lrp.2018.12.001

Wodarski, K., Wodarska, J., & Skubis, I. (2025). *Professional profile of a top manager in a process and project organization.* Scientific Papers of Silesian University of Technology. Organization and Management Series, No. 237.

Wołk, A., Skowrońska, H., & Skubis, I. (2021). Multilingual chatbot for e-commerce: Data generation and machine translation. In *PACIS 2021 Proceedings* (Paper 232, pp. 1–14).

Wołk, K., Wołk, A., Wnuk, D., Grześ, T., & Skubis, I. (2022). Survey on dialogue systems including Slavic languages. *Neurocomputing*, *497*, 62–84. https://doi.org/10.1016/j.neucom.2021.11.076

Artificial Intelligence as a Factor of Transformation, Innovation or a New Paradigm of Development in Entrepreneurship

1

1.1 INTRODUCTION

Artificial intelligence (AI) has become one of the key factors in civilisational change in the first decades of the 21st century, increasingly referred to as a "general-purpose technology" capable of influencing almost all areas of social and economic life. Its impact is not limited to specific sectors of the economy or selected technologies it systematically permeates business models, work organisation methods, market structures, decision-making processes in enterprises and the understanding of entrepreneurship as an economic and social phenomenon (Różanowski, 2007; Stylec-Szromek, 2018). Learning algorithms, natural language processing systems, robotics, and big

DOI:10.1201/9781042024131-2

data analysis form the basis of a new operating environment for companies, for which the ability to use artificial intelligence is becoming a prerequisite for maintaining competitiveness (Skalfist et al., 2020). Given the growing scale of the impact of artificial intelligence , a fundamental question arises: is artificial intelligence merely a factor of transformation, accelerating processes previously initiated by digitisation, automation, and globalisation, or is it a driver of radical innovation, leading to qualitative changes in the way products, services, and business models are created? (Datsenko, 2024). There is also increasing speculation about whether AI is transforming into a new paradigm of development – an interpretative and operational framework that redefines the foundations of entrepreneurship, as electricity, the steam engine and the internet did before it (Walicka & Czemiel-Grzybowska, 2023).

The aim of this chapter is to provide a multifaceted analysis of the role of artificial intelligence as a force shaping contemporary entrepreneurship. It covers both the theoretical dimension – defining AI, its classification, models of impact on businesses and the economy – and the practical dimension, covering specific areas of application, changes in management, marketing, finance, and production processes. The social, ethical, and legal consequences will also be considered, including the impact of artificial intelligence on the labour market, the structure of qualifications, the responsibility of algorithms, and data security. The introduction of artificial intelligence into business activities brings not only benefits but also challenges. These include high implementation costs, a shortage of specialists, the need to change organisational culture, the risk of job losses as a result of automation, and the problem of inequality in access to new technologies between large and small enterprises and between different regions of the world. At the same time, the dynamic development of artificial intelligence prompts reflection on the limits of its application, ethical responsibility, and the role of public regulation.

The main objective of this study is to provide a comprehensive analysis of the importance of artificial intelligence in the development and transformation of modern enterprises, with particular emphasis on its impact on business models, the level of innovation, and the shaping of a new paradigm of entrepreneurship. This approach is in line with research on AI-based business models as a key source of competitive advantage (Climent et al., 2024).

In this chapter, concepts such as paradigm, innovation, and transformation are not considered in the context of detailed analysis or terminological interpretation found in the literature on the subject. They have been adopted in accordance with their colloquial, commonly used meaning in everyday circulation.

The considerations presented are based on achievements in economics, innovation management, entrepreneurship theory, and social sciences. Their aim is not only to describe the current role of artificial intelligence, but also to attempt to predict its further impact on economic and social processes, and in particular on the way entrepreneurship is understood and practised in the coming decades. The risk associated with the lack of transparency of algorithms, as pointed out by O'Neill (2016), is becoming a key challenge for contemporary managers, requiring them to have not only technical knowledge but also ethical sensitivity (Floridi et al., 2018).

1.2 DEFINITIONAL SCOPE OF ARTIFICIAL INTELLIGENCE

Artificial intelligence is a complex, dynamic, and ambiguous concept, developing in parallel in many fields of science and economic practice (Jorzik et al., 2024). Broadly speaking, it refers to computer systems capable of performing tasks that require intelligence in humans, such as learning, reasoning, perception, adaptation to changing conditions, and decision-making (Climent et al., 2024). Modern AI systems can analyse huge data sets, recognise images and speech, generate text and images, recommend business solutions, and even conduct conversations, simulating communication between humans (Mhaskey, 2024). Key areas of AI application include natural language processing, machine learning and deep learning, pattern recognition, market behaviour forecasting, decision-making automation, robotisation, and content generation. The development of multilingual and multimodal models has led to a situation where artificial intelligence not only supports humans in data analysis, but is beginning to take over some cognitive activities, raising questions about the future role of humans in business and management (Hasan, 2025). The literature distinguishes between two basic types of artificial intelligence. The first is narrow artificial intelligence (ANI), which specialises in performing specific tasks such as image classification, demand forecasting, or customer service in the form of chatbots (Martinez, 2018). The second type is artificial general intelligence (AGI), a hypothetical system capable of performing a wide range of cognitive tasks at a human level. Although AGI remains a theoretical concept, the dynamic development of generated technologies and deep learning is gradually bringing us closer to more universal forms of machine intelligence (Sajja, 2020). To organise these concepts, they are presented in tabular form (Table 1.1):

The scope of artificial intelligence encompasses not only algorithms and computational models, but also technological infrastructure, data, learning processes, and the socio-economic context of its use. Artificial intelligence operates at the intersection of computer science, mathematics, statistics,

TABLE 1.1 Artificial intelligence in business practice: Classification and applications

TYPE OF AI	*CHARACTERISTICS*	*EXAMPLES OF APPLICATIONS*	*SIGNIFICANCE FOR ENTREPRENEURSHIP*
Narrow AI (ANI)	Performs single, specialised tasks	Recommendation systems, data analysis, chatbots, computer vision	Process automation, cost optimisation, decision support
General AI (AGI)	Hypothetical, with universal cognitive abilities	Currently no practical implementations	Potential paradigm shift in the labour market and management
Generative AI	Creates new content (text, images, sound, code)	Language models, creative AI tools	Product innovations, new business models, personalisation of offers

Source: Own work.

cognitive science, and management science, which makes its development interdisciplinary in nature (Cao, 2025). Data is a key element of modern artificial intelligence systems – both its quality and quantity determine the effectiveness of models. Without properly prepared data sets, even the most advanced algorithms are unable to generate valuable results, which is of significant importance for companies implementing artificial intelligence-based solutions. It is worth emphasising that artificial intelligence does not possess consciousness or intentionality in the human sense. Its "intelligence" is functional and statistical in nature, based on identifying patterns and probabilities in data, rather than understanding meaning or context in a human-specific way (Akhil et al., 2023). For this reason, artificial intelligence is a tool that supports decision-making processes rather than an autonomous substitute for them, which creates a need for human oversight (human-in-the-loop), especially in high-risk areas such as finance, medicine and human resource management (Abdussalam, 2024). Expanding the scope of classification, the concept of responsible artificial intelligence, which emphasises ethical, legal, and social issues, is also increasingly being highlighted (Carrillo, 2020). It covers issues such as the transparency of algorithms and the explanation of decisions made by artificial intelligence systems (explainable AI). For businesses, this means not only implementing innovative technologies, but also adapting them to legal regulations, such as the EU Artificial Intelligence Act, and building trust among customers and stakeholders. From an entrepreneurial perspective, artificial intelligence is becoming a competitive advantage, but at the same time a source of new organisational challenges. It requires investment in the digital skills of employees, changes in management models, and a redefinition of decision-making roles (Opolska-Bielańska, 2025). Artificial intelligence does not completely replace humans, but it changes the nature of work, shifting the emphasis from routine tasks to creative, strategic, and supervisory tasks. In this sense, the scope of artificial intelligence encompasses not only technology, but also the transformation of the way modern organisations and entire economic ecosystems function. AI does not fully replace humans, but changes the nature of work – shifting the emphasis from routine tasks to creative, strategic and supervisory ones. In this sense, the scope of artificial intelligence encompasses not only technology, but also the transformation of the way modern organisations and entire economic ecosystems function. Theoretical considerations to date point to the growing importance of artificial intelligence as a factor transforming modern entrepreneurship and organisational models. However, in order to place these conclusions in a broader scientific context and verify their consistency with existing research, it is reasonable to conduct an in-depth review of the literature on the subject. This literature allows us not only to identify the main trends in research on the impact of AI on entrepreneurship and innovation, but also to capture the evolution of theoretical approaches – from perceiving artificial intelligence as a tool for process automation to treating it as a general-purpose technology capable of redefining the logic of value creation in a data-driven economy. Early approaches to the relationship between technology and organisational innovation, although not directly related to artificial intelligence, provide an important theoretical background for analysing its contemporary implications. Christensen's (1997) concept of disruptive innovation suggests that new technologies can erode existing business models and competitive advantages, which is an important reference point for interpreting the impact of AI on companies operating in traditional sectors. Similarly, the concept of "general-purpose technology" presented by Brynjolfsson and McAfee (2014) allows artificial intelligence to be embedded in a broader process of long-term economic transformation, emphasising its potential to generate complementary innovations in many sectors simultaneously, which directly corresponds to the issue discussed in the chapter on the systemic nature of changes brought about by AI. This perspective is further developed in works focusing directly on artificial intelligence as a factor in changing business models and innovation processes. Bughin, Seong, Manyika, Chui, and Joshi (2018) point out that AI is becoming a source of a new wave of productivity and competitive advantage for companies, which necessitates the reorganisation of decision-making processes and organisational structures. In turn, the analysis conducted by Cockburn, Henderson, and Stern (2018) presents AI as a new "general-purpose factor" in the processes of discovering and commercialising innovation, which directly supports the thesis of the chapter on the role of artificial intelligence in accelerating the dynamics of technological entrepreneurship. This view is confirmed by the research of Agrawal, Gans, and Goldfarb (2019), who argue that the reduction in prediction costs thanks to AI leads to transformations in decision-making structures in organisations, thus influencing the way business models are designed and resources are allocated. The literature on entrepreneurship increasingly emphasises that artificial intelligence lowers barriers to market entry and changes the conditions for the creation of new ventures. Fossen and Sorgner (2019) point out that digital technologies, including AI-based solutions, foster the emergence of new forms of digital entrepreneurship, enabling individuals and small teams to compete with larger entities through access to advanced analytical and automation tools. This approach is further developed by Nambisan, Wright, and Feldman (2019), who describe digital entrepreneurship as a phenomenon embedded in platform ecosystems, where algorithms and data become key strategic resources. From the perspective of this chapter, these works provide a theoretical basis for analysing the transition from classical models of entrepreneurship to forms based on data and algorithmic infrastructure. Empirical research on the impact of AI on business innovation is also a significant trend in the literature. Research by Brynjolfsson, Rock, and Syverson (2021) shows that the implementation of digital technologies, including AI, is associated with a so-called productivity lag, which means that the full benefits of AI adoption only become apparent over a longer time horizon and require complementary organisational changes. In the context of this chapter, this conclusion allows us to take a critical look at narratives about the immediate effects of AI implementation and highlights the importance of institutional and competence factors. This approach is complemented by research by Autor, Levy, and Murnane (2003), which, although earlier, provides an analytical framework for interpreting the impact of automation on the structure of tasks at work, which has a direct impact on the analysis of changes in the competences of entrepreneurs and employees in the context of the growing role of AI. Critical works that allow entrepreneurial processes to be placed in a broader institutional context make a significant contribution to the discussion of the social and ethical implications of artificial intelligence. Crawford (2021) presents AI as a technology embedded in global power relations, resource exploitation, and social inequalities, which is an important addition to the chapter on the analysis of risks and social costs associated with the algorithmisation of economic processes. Similarly, O'Neill (2016) draws attention to the problem of algorithmic bias and its impact on organisational decisions, which is relevant for assessing the responsibility of companies implementing AI systems in areas such as recruitment, risk assessment, and customer segmentation. Floridi et al. (2018) propose an ethical framework for the development and implementation of AI, emphasising the need to integrate values such as transparency, responsibility, and fairness into innovation processes, which directly corresponds to the postulate of responsible technological entrepreneurship. The literature also emphasises the importance of competence and human capital in the processes of AI adaptation in organisations. The work of Autor (2015) indicates that digital technologies are changing the structure of demand for competences, increasing the importance of skills complementary to automation, such as creativity, complex problem solving, and managerial abilities. In the context of this chapter, these conclusions support the thesis that the competency profile of entrepreneurs needs to be redefined in a data-driven economy. This perspective is complemented by the analyses of Acemoglu and Restrepo (2020), which show the ambivalent impact of automation on employment and economic growth, allowing AI considerations to be placed in the broader debate on the relationship between technology and the labour market. A comprehensive review of the literature indicates that artificial intelligence functions in scientific research simultaneously as a tool for increasing efficiency, a factor accelerating innovation, and an element transforming the foundations of entrepreneurship. The integration of the work of authors such as Christensen (1997), Brynjolfsson and McAfee (2014), Cockburn et al. (2018), Agrawal et al. (2019), Nambisan et al. (2019), Fossen and Sorgner (2019), Brynjolfsson, Rock, and Syverson (2021), Acemoglu and Restrepo (2020), and Crawford (2021) allows us to place the impact of AI on entrepreneurship analysed in this chapter within a well-established theoretical and empirical framework. At the same time, this literature reveals significant research gaps, especially regarding the long-term effects of AI use on the sustainability of business models and technological inequalities between entities with diverse resources. In this sense, the literature review not only strengthens the chapter's argumentation, but also justifies the need for further research on the role of artificial intelligence as a factor shaping the future trajectories of entrepreneurship and innovation.

1.2.1 Research Methodology

The research strategy adopted in this chapter is multi-stage and interdisciplinary, allowing for a multidimensional approach to the issue of artificial intelligence in the context of the economy and entrepreneurship. The first stage involved a qualitative analysis of scientific literature, including publications in the fields of economics, management sciences, computer science and innovation studies. This analysis was supplemented by a review of industry reports and strategic documents prepared by international institutions, consulting firms, and research organisations, which allowed us to capture current trends and practical implications of the development of artificial intelligence-based technologies. Another element of the methodology will be a comparative analysis of the definitions of artificial intelligence used in various scientific disciplines. The aim of this stage was to identify similarities and differences in the ways of conceptualising AI, as well as to determine how different theoretical approaches influence the interpretation of its role in economic and organisational processes (Gartner, 2024; Jabeen et al., 2024). This analysis made it possible to develop a coherent conceptual framework as a basis for further research considerations. The theoretical research was supplemented by case studies of selected companies implementing AI-based solutions. Both large organisations and SMEs operating in various industries were analysed, which allowed for a comparison of the scale, objectives, and effects of AI implementation. The use of serious research methods enabled a comprehensive assessment of the role of artificial intelligence in the transformation of the modern economy (Cao, 2025; Jabeen et al., 2024). It should also be emphasised that the terms "paradigm shift" and "innovation" are not analysed in terms of their definitions; their meaning is taken from everyday usage in the literature on the subject. For the purposes of this study, the following research hypotheses were formulated:

H1: Artificial intelligence plays an important role as a factor in the transformation of enterprises, influencing changes in business models, organisational structures, and the implementation of operational processes.

H2: The use of artificial intelligence in enterprises contributes to an increase in the level of innovation, leading to the creation of new products, services, and sources of value creation.

H3: Artificial intelligence is a new paradigm for the development of entrepreneurship, fundamentally redefining the understanding of entrepreneurship, the functioning of markets, and the relationship between humans and technology.

The formulated hypotheses set the direction for further empirical analysis and provide the basis for interpreting the research results presented in the following sections of the thesis. Their verification will be carried out on the basis of the collected theoretical material and conclusions from case studies of enterprises using artificial intelligence solutions. The adopted research approach will not only enable the assessment of the scale of AI's impact on the functioning of organisations, but also the identification of mechanisms determining the transformation and innovation processes taking place in the modern economy. Thus, these hypotheses form an analytical framework for further considerations on the role of artificial intelligence in shaping new models of entrepreneurship.

1.2.2 A Comparative Analysis of Definitions of Artificial Intelligence Used in Various Scientific Disciplines

Previous considerations regarding the impact of artificial intelligence on entrepreneurship, innovation, and organisational transformation need to be supplemented with a more fundamental conceptual reflection. Before it is possible to fully grasp the mechanisms of AI's impact on economic and social processes, it is necessary to clarify the very meaning of the term "artificial intelligence", which, despite its widespread use, remains an ambiguous and multidimensional concept (Sajja, 2020). In scientific literature, it functions in parallel in various disciplines, each of which gives it a slightly different meaning, resulting from different research traditions, cognitive goals, and methodological tools. As a result, artificial intelligence is not a homogeneous object of analysis, but an interpretative category that takes on different meanings depending on the theoretical and application context. The lack of a uniform definition is not only a terminological problem, but has significant implications for the design of empirical research, the interpretation of results and the formulation of conclusions about the role of AI in the development of entrepreneurship. In technical sciences and computer science, artificial intelligence is primarily understood in functional terms, as the ability of computer systems to perform tasks that require intelligence in humans. Definitions derived from this approach focus on operational aspects such as machine learning, reasoning, pattern recognition, and decision optimisation under uncertainty. Intelligence here is instrumental in nature and is measured by the effectiveness of the system in a specific task environment. In this sense, artificial intelligence does not need to "understand" the meaning of the operations it performs, but only to generate accurate results based on data processing (Martinez, 2018). This approach favours a pragmatic view of AI as a utility technology whose value is assessed in terms of efficiency, scalability, and reliability. In the context of entrepreneurship, this means perceiving AI primarily as a tool for increasing productivity, automating decision-making processes, and supporting the management of complex information flows. Different emphases appear in cognitive science and cognitive psychology, where artificial intelligence is treated not only as an engineering technology, but also as a model of human cognitive processes. In this view, AI is a tool for simulating the mechanisms of perception, learning, memory, and reasoning, and its development is closely linked to the quest for a better understanding of the nature of the human mind. Definitions used in this area emphasise the similarity of the structures and mechanisms of artificial systems to human cognitive processes, even if this does not lead to maximum practical efficiency. From this perspective, artificial intelligence becomes not only a tool for optimising economic activities, but also a theoretical laboratory in which hypotheses about cognition, learning, and adaptation are tested. The consequence of this approach is a more cautious interpretation of AI capabilities, which are not treated as a substitute for human intelligence, but as its limited, functional imitation. Yet another definitional dimension appears in philosophical reflection, in which artificial intelligence is analysed in ontological and epistemological terms. In this vein, questions about whether machines can possess "intelligence" in a sense similar to humans, or whether they merely simulate intelligent behaviour, are of key importance. The distinction between so-called weak and strong artificial intelligence highlights the fact that algorithmic effectiveness does not necessarily imply the existence of understanding, consciousness, or intentionality. The philosophical perspective therefore problematises technical definitions of AI, pointing out that reducing intelligence to computational efficiency leads to a simplification of complex cognitive phenomena. In the context of entrepreneurship, this means maintaining a critical distance from the narrative of technological determinism, according to which AI systems would autonomously replace humans in decision-making processes in the future. The philosophical approach to artificial intelligence raises awareness of issues of responsibility, the meaning of decisions, and the limits of delegating cognitive power to algorithmic systems. In economics and management sciences, definitions of artificial intelligence shift the focus from the nature of intelligence to the function and effects of using technology in business. AI is seen here as a general-purpose technology capable of producing broad complementary effects in the form of increased productivity, the emergence of new business models, changes in the structure of employment, and the dynamics of market competition (Cao, 2025). In this view, artificial intelligence is defined primarily by its applications: process automation, predictive analytics, personalisation of offers, and support for managerial decisions. Algorithmic intelligence is not an end in itself here, but a means to increase economic efficiency and create new value. This approach encourages the treatment of AI as a strategic resource, the possession and skilful use of which can determine the competitive advantage of enterprises. At the same time, the economic approach to defining AI often overlooks deeper cognitive and ethical issues, focusing on the measurable results of technological implementations. The social science perspective adds an additional dimension to the definitional analysis of artificial intelligence, viewing it as part of broader processes of social, cultural, and institutional transformation. In this view, AI is not a neutral technical tool, but a technology embedded in specific power relations, economic interests, and institutional structures. Definitions in this area emphasise the role of algorithms in shaping individual behaviour, mechanisms of social control, knowledge distribution and the reproduction of inequalities (Crawford,

2021; O'Neill, 2016). Artificial intelligence appears to be a technology that co-creates social order, rather than just a set of algorithms performing specific functions. In the context of entrepreneurship, this approach raises awareness of the fact that the implementation of AI is not a purely technical process, but has specific social consequences, including changes in labour relations, information asymmetries, and potential forms of digital exclusion. A comparative analysis of the definitions of artificial intelligence used in various scientific disciplines therefore allows us to conclude that this concept is relational and contextual in nature. The common denominator of all approaches is the belief that AI refers to systems capable of processing information in an adaptive manner that goes beyond simple, rigid programming rules. The differences concern the interpretation of "intelligence" itself – in technical approaches, it is functional and instrumental in nature, in cognitive science it refers to the modelling of cognitive processes, in philosophy it becomes an ontological problem, in economics – a strategic resource, and in social sciences – an element of broader structures of power and social relations. The integration of these perspectives allows for a more adequate understanding of the complex nature of artificial intelligence as a phenomenon that is simultaneously technological, cognitive, economic, and social. Such an interdisciplinary synthesis is an essential starting point for further analysis of the impact of AI on entrepreneurship, innovation, and the shaping of new models of development in an economy based on data and algorithms.

1.2.3 Analysis of Reports and Strategic Documentation Developed by International Institutions, Consulting firms, and Research Organisations

The development of artificial intelligence as a technological phenomenon of global significance is strongly reflected in numerous analyses, industry reports, and strategic documents prepared by international organisations and intergovernmental platforms. These documents not only map the current state of knowledge about AI, but also indicate directions for future changes in the areas of entrepreneurship, the labour market, public policy, and ethical standards. One of the key sources of analysis is the publication "Artificial Intelligence in Society" prepared by the OECD, which is a pioneering attempt to describe the impact of artificial intelligence on various sectors of the economy and society. The report indicates that AI contributes to economic and social transformation, while raising questions about public policy in the areas of efficiency, privacy, security, and social justice. The OECD documents the rapid growth of private investment in AI and the growing role of start-ups in this area, highlighting national differences in the level of technology adoption and the need for coordinated legislative and educational action. OECD reports also systematically address the adoption of AI technologies in business practice. New data published by the organisation indicates that the percentage of companies using AI is growing rapidly, meaning that these technologies are no longer the preserve of high-tech companies and are beginning to penetrate sectors that have been less digitally advanced to date. The OECD report once again outlines the challenges related to employee skills and adaptation barriers that must be taken into account by policy makers and business leaders. In 2025, the OECD and the World Economic Forum also published a report entitled "AI in Strategic Foresight: Reshaping Anticipatory Governance", which emphasises the importance of artificial intelligence not only as a technological tool, but also as a factor influencing strategic management processes in the public and private sectors. The document indicates that AI can help institutions anticipate trends, improve policy planning, and identify future risks and opportunities. It is worth noting that the report presents AI as an element of building anticipatory strategies that go beyond current decision-making cycles, which is particularly important for companies planning long-term investments in innovation. The strategic documents prepared by the OECD complement the initiatives of other entities. An example is the report prepared by the World Economic Forum in collaboration with KPMG, entitled "Blueprint for Intelligent Economies: AI Competitiveness through Regional Collaboration". This document presents AI as a key element of the fourth industrial revolution, emphasising that responsible implementation of technology and regional cooperation are the foundation for building innovative, resilient, and competitive economies of the future. The authors of the report point out that implementations should bring benefits not only in terms of increased operational efficiency, but also through the creation of new business models and improved quality of life for citizens. In addition, the report emphasises the role of ethics, data quality, and sustainable infrastructure as key components of these strategies. In a similar vein, global organisations are launching initiatives that combine ethical issues with practical implementation challenges. Through the Business Council for Ethics of AI, UNESCO promotes responsible practices in the private sector, emphasising the need to take human values and human rights into account in the development and use of AI systems. Such documents and platforms for cross-sector dialogue indicate that the discussion on AI is not limited to technical aspects, but also covers social, cultural, and ethical issues that are crucial from the perspective of companies implementing AI outside of state-of-the-art research laboratories. Outside the framework of the OECD and the WEF, the International AI Safety Report, the first independent international AI safety report, which assesses a wide range of risks associated with general-purpose AI systems, is also of significant importance. This document was commissioned by the countries participating in the AI Safety Summit and is intended to serve as a basis for discussion on global safety mechanisms, which, from a business perspective, means that issues of control, oversight, and responsibility for decisions made by intelligent systems must be taken into account. It is also worth mentioning the working documents and analyses supporting the preparation of research ecosystems and national policies integrating AI into research and innovation activities. The report "Preparing national research ecosystems for AI: strategies and progress" points to the diverse approaches of countries to building AI infrastructure, the need for international cooperation and the need to exchange experiences, which is a prerequisite for the effective use of AI in businesses, especially in the context of innovation development and research commercialisation. An analysis of these strategic documents and industry reports reveals several common themes that are key to understanding the role of artificial intelligence in entrepreneurship and innovation. First, there is broad recognition that AI has the potential to significantly increase the productivity and competitiveness of companies, as reflected in OECD statistics and reports by the WEF and KPMG. Secondly, these documents consistently emphasise that the creation of regulatory frameworks, ethical norms, and safety standards is essential to ensure that the benefits of AI are sustainable and accessible to various economic actors. Thirdly, many reports point to a competence barrier – a lack of skilled personnel and unequal access to AI technology, which may limit the ability of smaller enterprises to fully adapt AI solutions. In summary, international reports and policy documents indicate that artificial intelligence is not just a technological curiosity, but a key driver of economic and social change. Their analyses provide both a map of current trends and guidance on public policies and management practices that can support businesses in the effective and responsible use of AI. Such documents are a complementary source of knowledge, combining technical, economic, and ethical perspectives and creating a framework in which AI-based innovations can contribute to sustainable economic development (Kuang et al., 2015).

1.3 TECHNOLOGICAL COMPONENTS OF ARTIFICIAL INTELLIGENCE

Artificial intelligence is not a homogeneous technology, but a complex set of IT, algorithmic, and infrastructure solutions that together form the basis of today's digital transformation. Its technological components have developed gradually, responding to growing computing capabilities, data availability, and the economy's demand for automation and intelligent decision-making support (Sajja, 2020). In business terms, this means that AI is no longer the domain of research laboratories, but has become an integral part of business strategies and a source of competitive advantage. Machine learning remains at the heart of artificial intelligence architecture, enabling IT systems to adapt to changing market conditions without the need to manually programme each scenario. Machine learning algorithms learn from historical data, allowing companies to identify hidden relationships, predict trends, and optimise decisions in real time. In business practice, this technology is used in areas such as dynamic pricing, fraud detection, supply chain management, and personalisation of commercial offers. Its importance lies in its ability to scale organisational knowledge and transform data into a strategic resource. Deep learning has developed on the basis of machine learning, which, thanks to the use of multi-layer neural networks, enables the analysis of highly complex data. Unlike traditional algorithms, deep learning systems are able to create data representations on their own, which significantly increases their effectiveness in tasks requiring pattern recognition. In the context of entrepreneurship, this means the possibility of automating processes that were previously considered too complex or costly to be performed by machines, such as medical image analysis, customer emotion recognition, and market behaviour prediction (Beraja et al., 2023). An integral component of modern AI systems is natural language processing, which enables machines to understand and generate text and speech in a manner similar to humans. Developments in this field have led to the creation of intelligent assistants, chatbots, and document analysis systems that are significantly changing the way businesses communicate with their stakeholders. From a business perspective, NLP technologies enable the automation of customer service, analysis of market opinions and sentiments, and support for management processes through the rapid processing of large volumes of text information. At the same time, computer vision is developing, enabling machines to interpret visual data and make decisions based on it. This technology is widely used in sectors such as industry, retail, and transport, where it is used to monitor production processes, analyse consumer behaviour, and support autonomous systems (Schank, 1991). Computer vision increases the precision and speed of business operations, while reducing the risk of human error and operating costs. Robotics, as a combination of artificial intelligence and physical systems, represents the next stage in the evolution of automation. Modern robots, equipped with learning algorithms and perception systems, are capable of adaptive operation in a changing environment. In the context of entrepreneurship, their application goes beyond traditional manufacturing, encompassing logistics, agriculture, healthcare, and the service sector. The development of intelligent robotics is leading to transformations in the organisational structure of enterprises and a redefinition of the relationship between capital and labour. Recommendation and prediction systems, which are based on the analysis of user behaviour and historical data, are also an important element of the artificial intelligence ecosystem. These systems are the foundation of digital platforms, influencing the way demand, consumer preferences and marketing strategies are shaped. In business terms, their importance lies in the ability to precisely tailor offerings to individual customer needs, leading to an increase in the value of market relationships and sales efficiency (Jabeen et al., 2024; Climent et al., 2024). The most advanced and rapidly developing component of artificial intelligence is generative AI, which enables the creation of new content and solutions based on input data. Unlike traditional analytical systems, generative AI not only interprets reality, but also actively co-creates it by generating texts, images, design models, and programming code. From an entrepreneurial perspective, this technology opens up new opportunities for product innovation, shortening development cycles, and reducing research and development costs. It is worth noting that the individual components of artificial intelligence function in close synergy, complementing and reinforcing each other. Their integration leads to the creation of complex systems that can autonomously analyse data, communicate with users, make decisions, and carry out actions in the physical world (Whittaker, 2018). For businesses, this means the need for a holistic approach to AI implementation, taking into account technological, organisational, ethical, and strategic aspects. In summary, the technological components of artificial intelligence are the foundation of a profound transformation of modern entrepreneurship. Their development not only increases the operational efficiency and innovation of enterprises, but also leads to a redefinition of business models, organisational structures, and the role of humans in economic processes. In this sense, artificial intelligence appears not as a single technological tool, but as a comprehensive system capable of transforming the logic of how markets and organisations function (Jabeen et al., 2024).

1.4 ENTREPRENEURSHIP IN THE AGE OF AI: A NEW PARADIGM OF ENTREPRENEURSHIP

The dynamic development of artificial intelligence is leading to a significant revision of existing concepts of entrepreneurship, which for a long time have focused on the role of the individual, material capital, and the ability to identify and exploit market opportunities. In a data- and algorithm-driven economy, traditional approaches prove insufficient to fully describe the processes of creating and developing business ventures. Entrepreneurship in the AI era is increasingly analysed as a systemic phenomenon, embedded in technological networks, innovation ecosystems and relationships between humans and intelligent systems. New theoretical approaches emphasise that data, the ability to process it, and the competence to design and use algorithms are becoming key entrepreneurial resources. Entrepreneurs are no longer solely initiators of innovation, but increasingly act as architects of technological solutions, integrators of systems, and coordinators of processes based on artificial intelligence. In this context, entrepreneurship is not just about responding to existing market needs, but about actively co-creating them through the analysis of behaviour patterns, trend prediction, and the personalisation of offers on a scale that was previously unattainable (W.I, 2018). The literature also increasingly emphasises a shift in focus from the individual characteristics of entrepreneurs to organisational and relational skills. Effective use of AI requires access to technological infrastructure, cooperation with digital solution providers, participation in innovation ecosystems, and knowledge management skills. Entrepreneurship in the AI era is becoming a collective process in which value is created at the intersection of human competence, technology, and data. At the same time, new theoretical approaches draw attention to the growing importance of ethical, regulatory, and social issues. Decisions made with the support of algorithms affect not only economic efficiency, but also relationships with customers, employees, and society (Artificial, 2022). Responsible entrepreneurship in the AI era therefore requires consideration of algorithm transparency, data protection, and the impact of technology on the labour market and social inequalities. The theoretical approaches presented here provide a starting point for further consideration of the specific mechanisms by which artificial intelligence affects entrepreneurship (Cao, 2025; Hasan, 2025). In the following sections of this paper, the analysis will be deepened by discussing the entrepreneur as an agent of innovation in digital conditions, the development of algorithmic entrepreneurship, and the role of AI as a factor of transformation and innovation in economic practice (Kugan, et al., 2014). This approach will show how theoretical concepts are reflected in the real strategies and activities of companies operating in the era of artificial intelligence.

1.4.1 The Entrepreneur as an Agent of Innovation

In classical theories of entrepreneurship, the entrepreneur was seen as the central actor in the economic process, responsible for initiating change, organising resources, and taking risks in conditions of uncertainty. In the Schumpeterian tradition, they played the role of innovators who, by introducing "new combinations" of production factors, disrupted the existing market equilibrium and triggered a process of creative destruction. In Kirzner's approach, on the other hand, the entrepreneur was seen as an actor alert to market opportunities, able to spot information gaps and exploit imperfections in the price mechanism. In both of these approaches, human perception, intuition, creativity, and the ability to make decisions in situations of limited information played a key role (Kugan, et al., 2014). However, the development of artificial intelligence introduces a qualitatively new element to these classical approaches, leading to a transformation of the very ontology of entrepreneurship. Increasingly, innovation is no longer the exclusive product of the human mind, but is becoming the result of interactions between humans and algorithmic systems that can analyse vast amounts of data, identify patterns invisible to human perception, and generate recommendations for product development, markets, and strategies. The entrepreneur is no longer the sole "bearer of market knowledge" but operates in an environment where some cognitive functions are delegated to machines (Agrawal, Gans, and Goldfarb, 2019; Cao, 2025). In this new context, entrepreneurs increasingly play the role of innovation system architects, technology integrators and managers of relationships between data, algorithms and human capital. Their task is not only to generate ideas, but also to design processes in which artificial intelligence can be effectively used to explore new market opportunities. This means a shift from entrepreneurship based on individual intuition to entrepreneurship based on the ability to configure complex technological systems. In this context, the issue of data as a basic production resource takes on particular importance. In an industrial economy, physical capital plays a key role, in a knowledge-based economy human capital, while in an algorithmic economy, data becomes the central resource. Entrepreneurs operate in an environment where information flows are continuously generated by users, sensors, Internet of Things devices, and digital platforms. The ability to acquire, integrate, cleanse, and analyse this data is becoming one of the main sources of competitive advantage. In this sense, entrepreneurs in the AI era are not only innovators, but also curators of data and analytical models. At the same time, the nature of business decisions is changing. Traditionally, strategic decisions were made based on limited information, managerial experience and cognitive heuristics. In the AI era, they are increasingly supported or partially replaced by predictive systems that analyse historical and current data in real time, forecast demand, optimise prices, and simulate the effects of alternative strategic scenarios (Agrawal, Gans, and Goldfarb, 2019; Mhaskey, 2024). This leads to a shift from intuitive entrepreneurship to algorithmic entrepreneurship, where the effectiveness of actions depends on the quality of models, the accuracy of input data, and the organisation's ability to learn from feedback. However, this does not mean that the role of humans is marginalised. On the contrary, the role of the entrepreneur is being redefined and becoming more complex. In the context of the growing autonomy of AI systems, their task is to formulate goals, interpret the results generated by algorithms, make sense of information, and make final decisions in ambiguous situations fraught with risk and ethical consequences. The entrepreneur thus becomes a "meta-decision-making" actor who does not so much decide on specific operational actions as on how and to what extent these decisions can be delegated to machines. In this context, the issue of responsibility for decisions made by AI systems takes on particular importance. In the traditional model of entrepreneurship, responsibility for success or failure rested unequivocally with the entrepreneur. In the algorithm-based model, this boundary becomes blurred: decisions are the result of complex statistical models, often opaque even to their creators. Entrepreneurs must therefore not only understand the logic of AI systems, but also take responsibility for their social, legal, and economic consequences, which introduces a new ethical dimension to the theory of entrepreneurship (Furman & Seamans, 2019). Artificial intelligence also influences the very process of innovation. Increasingly, innovation is continuous and iterative rather than disruptive. Algorithmic models are constantly updated based on new data, leading to the permanent optimisation of products, services, and processes. Entrepreneurs are no longer the initiators of single breakthrough changes, but are beginning to act as managers of a dynamic innovation system that evolves in real time. Finally, the social dimension of entrepreneurship is also changing. The development of AI lowers the barriers to entry into many markets, enabling small businesses and start-ups to use advanced analytical and generative tools without having to incur huge capital expenditure. At the same time, it promotes the concentration of economic power in the hands of entities with the largest data sets and the most advanced computing infrastructure. Entrepreneurs therefore operate in a deeply ambivalent environment, in which AI simultaneously democratises access to innovation and deepens competitive inequalities. In this sense, entrepreneurs in the age of artificial intelligence appear as a new type of innovator: not only creators of products and services, but also designers of relationships between people, algorithms, and markets (Yu, et al., 2018). Entrepreneurship is no longer solely the domain of individual creativity, but is becoming systemic, networked, and co-evolutionary. This shift is one of the key arguments in favour of the thesis that artificial intelligence not only transforms entrepreneurship, but also redefines its theoretical foundations, introducing a new logic of value creation in the 21st century economy.

1.4.2 Digital and Algorithmic Entrepreneurship

The dynamic development of digital technologies, particularly artificial intelligence, is leading to the emergence of new forms of entrepreneurship, referred to as digital and algorithmic entrepreneurship. Unlike traditional business models, in which material resources, production infrastructure, and financial capital played a key role, modern entrepreneurship increasingly relies on intangible resources such as data, knowledge, software, and the ability to design and implement algorithms (Coeckelbergh, 2020). In this approach, the essence of entrepreneurial activity becomes the creation of value through information processing and the automation of decision-making processes. Algorithmic entrepreneurship focuses on the design, training and implementation of artificial intelligence models that form the core of the products or services offered. In this model, the entrepreneur acts as an architect of algorithmic systems, responsible for designing data flows, integrating different technologies and ensuring consistency between the technical layer and the business objectives of the organisation. The ability to identify market problems that can be solved through automation, prediction, or AI-based personalisation is crucial. In algorithmic entrepreneurship, the value creation process is based on continuous learning by systems, which means that the product or service is not static but evolves as new data becomes available. The entrepreneur therefore does not sell a one-off solution, but offers a dynamic service whose quality depends on the effectiveness of the business models. This encourages the emergence of new forms of monetisation, based, among other things, on subscriptions, "as-a-service" models, digital platforms, and ecosystems based on data sharing (Campolo et al., 2017). A distinctive feature of algorithmic entrepreneurship is the strong link between economic activity and digital infrastructure. Access to computing power, cloud computing, programming tools, and global technology platforms is becoming a prerequisite for doing business on an international scale. At the same time, there is a significant increase in system interoperability, data security, and regulatory compliance, which requires entrepreneurs to have skills that go beyond traditional business management. The shift in emphasis from physical capital-based entrepreneurship to knowledge-, data- and software-based entrepreneurship is changing the barriers to market entry. On the one hand, it lowers them, enabling start-ups and small businesses to access advanced technologies without the need for their own infrastructure. On the other hand, it promotes the concentration of economic power in the hands of entities with the largest data sets and the most developed technological ecosystems (Millington, 2019). Algorithmic entrepreneurship therefore operates in the tension between the decentralisation of innovation and its platformisation. The development of digital and algorithmic entrepreneurship also affects the relationship between the entrepreneur and the market. The traditional model, in which entrepreneurs responded to market signals with a certain delay, is being replaced by a model based on real-time data analysis. Algorithms enable dynamic adjustment of prices, offers, and marketing strategies to changing customer preferences, leading to the emergence of so-called reactive and predictive entrepreneurship. In this approach, a company's competitiveness depends not so much on the physical speed of production as on the speed of information processing. At the same time, algorithmic entrepreneurship raises new ethical and social challenges. The automation of decisions can lead to a lack of transparency in algorithmic discrimination processes and a reduction in user autonomy. Entrepreneurs must therefore take responsibility not only for the economic efficiency of the solutions they offer, but also for their compliance with social, legal, and ethical standards. In this sense, digital and algorithmic entrepreneurship requires a new approach to management, based on responsible technology design and conscious shaping of the relationship between algorithms and users (Deborah, Verdicchio, 2017). In summary, digital and algorithmic entrepreneurship is one of the most dynamically developing forms of economic activity in the modern economy. Its essence is to create value through data, algorithms, and automation, which leads to a profound transformation of business models, innovation processes, and the role of the entrepreneur. This phenomenon reinforces the thesis that artificial intelligence not only supports entrepreneurship, but is becoming one of its key foundations, shaping a new logic for the functioning of enterprises in the 21st century economy.

1.5 ARTIFICIAL INTELLIGENCE AS A FACTOR IN BUSINESS TRANSFORMATION

AI is playing an increasingly important role in business transformation processes, constituting one of the key elements in adapting organisations to the conditions of a dynamically changing economic environment. Unlike earlier stages of technological development, where innovations were primarily supportive or improving selected areas of activity, AI is increasingly influencing the overall functioning of enterprises. Its impact covers both the operational and strategic spheres, leading to gradual but profound changes in organisational structures, decision-making processes, and relations with the market environment. The transformative nature of artificial intelligence is manifested primarily in its ability to integrate dispersed data and transform it into useful knowledge. Companies that implement AI-based solutions are able to respond more quickly to changes in demand, optimise resource utilisation, and improve risk management. In this sense, artificial intelligence becomes a tool that supports the adaptability of organisations, allowing them to make decisions in conditions of high uncertainty and complexity. At the same time, AI is changing the logic of how companies operate, shifting the focus from reactive to proactive and predictive approaches. The use of learning algorithms not only enables the analysis of past data, but also the prediction of future events and the simulation of various development scenarios. As a result, companies can shape their strategies based on forecasts and models, rather than solely on the experience of managers or decision-making intuition. The transformation of companies under the influence of artificial intelligence also has a cultural and organisational dimension (D'Alfonso, 2020). Implementing AI-based solutions requires a change in the way we think about work, responsibility, and collaboration within an organisation. A data-driven culture, openness to experimentation, and a willingness to learn and adapt are becoming increasingly important. Companies that are able to combine the technological potential of artificial intelligence with the development of employee competencies and appropriate leadership achieve greater capacity for sustainable transformation. In the context of earlier considerations regarding entrepreneurship in the AI era, artificial intelligence appears not only as a tool for improving the functioning of organisations, but also as an important factor in redefining the way value is created. The transformation of enterprises is becoming a multidimensional process, encompassing technological, organisational, and social changes. In the following sections of this paper, this analysis will be elaborated upon by discussing specific areas of transformation, such as internal processes, employee roles and the strategic consequences of AI implementation, which will allow for a better understanding of the mechanisms and scope of artificial intelligence's impact on contemporary enterprises (Kajta, et al., 2025).

1.5.1 Transformation of Internal Business Processes

One of the fundamental areas of impact of artificial intelligence in enterprises is the transformation of internal processes, understood as the gradual transformation of the ways in which operational, administrative, and decision-making activities are carried out. Unlike traditional automation, which is based on rigid rules and programmed sequences of actions, AI-based solutions are characterised by their ability to learn, adapt and analyse data in real time. This makes it possible not only to speed up processes, but also to optimise them on an ongoing basis. Artificial intelligence enables companies to automate a wide range of routine and repetitive tasks that previously required significant human resources. This applies in particular to accounting, billing, reporting, and administrative processes. AI-based systems can independently classify documents, detect irregularities, generate financial reports, and identify anomalies in data. This leads to a reduction in the number of errors, shorter task completion times and increased process transparency. At the same time, artificial intelligence has a significant impact on the quality and speed of analytical processes. Learning algorithms are capable of processing huge volumes of data from various sources, such as ERP and CRM systems, e-commerce platforms, and social media (Acemoglu, 2021). This enables companies to perform advanced predictive analytics, forecast demand, optimise supply chains and improve inventory management. Decisions based on such analyses are more accurate, less subjective, and better adapted to dynamically changing market conditions. However, in many cases, the transformation of internal processes is streamlining rather than revolutionary. AI is often implemented by gradually replacing or supporting existing tools, without fundamentally changing the organisational structure or business model of the company (Kit, 2023). The organisation becomes more efficient and flexible, but its basic operating logic remains unchanged. For this reason, artificial intelligence in this sense acts as an operational transformation factor that prepares the company for potentially deeper changes in the future.

1.5.2 Transformation of Employee Roles

The implementation of artificial intelligence in companies has an impact on the structure of employment and the nature of the work performed. The automation of processes based on clearly defined rules leads to a gradual reduction in the need for routine and repetitive work, both in the administrative and operational areas. At the same time, the importance of roles requiring skills that are difficult to fully automate is growing. The transformation of employee roles consists primarily in shifting the emphasis from performing operational tasks to supervising, interpreting, and improving them. Employees are increasingly acting as users and controllers of AI systems, responsible for verifying the results generated by algorithms, identifying potential errors, and assessing their compliance with the organisation's objectives. This requires the development of analytical skills, data handling skills, and a basic understanding of how algorithms work (Ransbotham, et al., 2019). At the same time, the importance of soft and creative skills, such as critical thinking, problem solving, communication, and empathy, is increasing. In areas requiring customer contact, team management or strategic decision-making, the role of humans remains crucial. Artificial intelligence serves as a supporting tool, providing recommendations and analyses, but does not replace human responsibility for final decisions. The transformation of employee roles also requires continuous improvement of qualifications and lifelong learning. Companies implementing AI must invest in the development of their employees' digital skills, create training programs, and support adaptation to new technologies. Failure to do so may lead to deepening skills gaps, resistance to change and reduced effectiveness of the solutions implemented. From an organisational perspective, the change in employee roles fosters new forms of human–technology collaboration. Work teams are increasingly interdisciplinary, combining technical, analytical, and managerial skills. Employees become part of a broader decision-making system in which artificial intelligence plays the role of a co-participant in the process, rather than just a tool. Such a model of cooperation requires a clear definition of responsibilities, transparency of algorithms, and consideration of ethical aspects. In summary, the transformation of employee roles brought about by artificial intelligence does not mean simply replacing humans with machines, but leads to a profound change in the nature of work. Humans cease to be performers of repetitive tasks and become interpreters, supervisors, and co-creators of AI-supported processes. This change is one of the key challenges and opportunities for modern enterprises, determining their ability to adapt in conditions of dynamic technological transformation (Panigutti et al., 2023).

1.6 ARTIFICIAL INTELLIGENCE AS A DRIVER OF INNOVATION

Artificial intelligence is one of the most important drivers of innovation in the modern economy. Unlike many earlier technologies, it does not only support production or management processes, but is increasingly becoming a key element in value creation. Its ability to learn from data, adapt to changing conditions and autonomously generate solutions means that AI-based innovations are both incremental and radical in nature. In this context, artificial intelligence not only accelerates the pace of innovation, but also changes its nature, shifting the focus from material resources to knowledge, data, and algorithms (Passi & Vorvoreanu, 2022).

1.6.1 Product Innovation

One of the most visible areas of artificial intelligence's impact is product innovation. AI-based products differ from traditional solutions in that they are not static – their functionality can evolve over time as new data becomes available. This means that the value of a product is not determined solely at the design stage, but also arises during its use. Intelligent assistants are an example of products in which AI plays a central role. Thanks to natural language processing and machine learning, they are able to engage in dialogue with the user, understand context, and learn preferences (Kleiber, 2024). In business, these types of assistants support time management, customer service, data analysis, and operational planning. Their innovation lies not only in the automation of communication, but also in their ability to personalise and continuously improve the quality of interactions. Predictive applications using AI algorithms enable the forecasting of customer behaviour, market trends, technical failures, and product demand (Konopka, 2023). Unlike traditional analytical tools, these systems can analyse huge volumes of data in real time and identify patterns that are invisible to humans. The innovation of such products lies in the shift from reactive to proactive decision-making, which significantly increases the competitiveness of companies. In the healthcare sector, artificial intelligence enables the creation of medical products tailored to the individual characteristics of the patient. Algorithms that analyse genetic data, medical history, and diagnostic test results allow for the design of personalised therapies and accurate predictions of treatment effectiveness. In this case, product innovation is not only about new technology, but also about a change in the philosophy of healthcare delivery – from a mass model to an individualised model. Artificial intelligence enables the creation of educational products that tailor content, learning pace, and teaching methods to the individual needs of the user. These systems analyse learning progress, identify areas for improvement, and autonomously modify the educational path. The innovation lies in moving away from a uniform curriculum in favour of personalised educational experiences, which increases learning effectiveness and motivation (Lizak, 2025). Generative artificial intelligence enables the creation of content such as text, images, music, and graphic designs. These tools are becoming products in their own right, used in marketing, media, design, and the entertainment industry. Their innovation lies in the democratisation of the creative process – lowering barriers to entry and accelerating the creation process. In this context, AI becomes a co-creator of value, rather than just a tool to support human work. Artificial intelligence also has a significant impact on the service sector, which accounts for the majority of added value in developed economies. AI-based service innovations focus on improving customer service quality, increasing the flexibility of the offer and optimising processes. By analysing behavioural, transactional, and contextual data, AI enables the creation of offers precisely tailored to individual customer needs (Raszyd, Wesołowska, Tomaszewska, 2024). Hyper-personalisation goes beyond traditional market segmentation, allowing each customer to be treated as a separate segment. The innovation of this approach lies in increasing value for the customer while simultaneously increasing sales efficiency. AI algorithms enable dynamic pricing based on demand, supply, competitor behaviour, and customer profile. Such solutions are used, among others, in e-commerce, transport, and the hotel industry. The innovation lies in moving away from rigid pricing models in favour of flexible strategies that respond to market changes in real time. AI-based chatbots and virtual consumers enable round-the-clock customer service. These systems are capable of solving standard problems, answering questions and redirecting more complex issues to employees. The innovation lies in combining high availability with reduced operating costs. In the industrial sector, AI enables the provision of predictive maintenance services (Patkowska, Zieliński, 2024). Analysis of data from sensors allows for the prediction of failures and the planning of maintenance at the optimal time. This approach reduces downtime, lowers cost, and increases safety. This is an example of service innovation that directly affects the efficiency of production processes. The development of AI has led to the emergence of new business models, such as “AI as a Service” and “Data as a Service” (Bortnowska, 2024). Companies can use advanced algorithms without having to develop them themselves, which lowers barriers to entry and promotes the development of innovative entrepreneurship.

1.6.2 Organisational and Model Innovations

In addition to products and services, artificial intelligence also influences the way companies are organised and business models are designed. In this area, innovations are structural and strategic in nature. AI enables the creation of business models based on platforms and data ecosystems. Companies no longer sell only products or services, but also access to algorithms, analyses, and predictions. Value is created in a network of connections between users, data, and technology. Thanks to AI, it is possible to autonomously collect, organise, and analyse organisational knowledge. Recommendation systems support decision-making, and intelligent knowledge bases enable faster access to information. Innovation consists in increasing the organisation’s ability to learn and adapt (Kowalik, 2024). Companies using AI often take the form of so-called “light” organisations, characterised by a small number of employees and a high level of automation. This allows them to quickly scale their operations and respond flexibly to market changes. One of the key aspects of organisational innovation is the transition from intuitive to algorithmic decision-making. AI enables real-time data analysis and supports managers in choosing optimal strategies. This leads to the emergence of companies designed from the outset to be data-driven, where data is a fundamental strategic resource (Bielińska-Dusza, 2022).

1.7 ARTIFICIAL INTELLIGENCE AS A NEW PARADIGM FOR DEVELOPMENT

In a situation where artificial intelligence is not limited to improving existing processes or supporting the creation of new products and services, but begins to fundamentally influence the way we perceive the economy, organisations, and entrepreneurship, it becomes reasonable to treat it as a new paradigm of development. This means moving away from traditional growth models based mainly on physical capital and human labour towards a logic in which data, algorithms, and the ability of systems to learn and adapt independently play a key role. Central to this paradigm is the role of data as a fundamental economic resource. Data is becoming not only a raw material used in decision-making processes, but also a source of value creation in itself. Its collection, processing, and interpretation using advanced algorithms enable the generation of knowledge, the prediction of market behaviour and the personalisation of products and services on an unprecedented scale (Walicka & Czemiel-Grzybowska, 2023). As a result, the competitive advantage of companies increasingly depends not on their physical assets, but on the quality of their data and their ability to use it effectively. Another important feature of the new paradigm is cognitive automation, which involves delegating tasks requiring analysis, reasoning, and decision-making to AI systems. Learning algorithms are able to independently identify patterns, optimise processes, and modify their behaviour in response to changing environmental conditions. This leads to the emergence of dynamic, self-learning systems that function continuously and adaptively, often beyond direct human control. In this context, the relationship between humans and technology is undergoing a fundamental change. Entrepreneurship in the new paradigm is based on human–machine collaboration, where decisions are made based on the synergies of human creativity, intuition, and responsibility with the analytical capabilities of AI systems (Kłoczko, 2024). The role of the entrepreneur is not only to use technology, but to consciously design, supervise, and integrate it with organisational goals and social values. The new development paradigm also means a shift in the economy towards business models based on algorithms and digital platforms. Value is increasingly created through intelligent automation, scalable predictive models and the ability to manage complex data ecosystems. Entrepreneurs operate not only in traditional goods and services markets, but also in information, attention, and model markets, where competition is about the ability to attract users, interpret data, and transform it into useful solutions. At the same time, operating in such a paradigm involves new forms of risk, referred to as algorithmic risk. This includes, among other things, data errors, algorithmic bias, lack of transparency in decision-making processes, and the unpredictability of learning systems. The ability to identify, assess, and manage these risks is becoming an important element of entrepreneurial competence, determining the sustainability and responsibility of development. In summary, artificial intelligence as a new paradigm of development not only redefines the mechanisms of value creation, but also changes the way we think about entrepreneurship, work, and market relations (Weinert, 2024). In this context, entrepreneurship becomes a process of designing and managing intelligent systems capable of continuous learning and adaptation. It is this ability to function in conditions of high complexity and dynamic change that forms the foundation for the development of enterprises in the era of artificial intelligence.

1.8 APPLICATIONS OF ARTIFICIAL INTELLIGENCE IN SELECTED SECTORS OF THE ECONOMY

Artificial intelligence is finding increasingly widespread application in various sectors of the economy, becoming an important factor in improving the efficiency, innovation, and adaptability of organisations. Its universal nature means that AI-based solutions can be used both in traditional sectors and in areas based on knowledge and creativity. This chapter discusses selected sectors of the economy in which the use of artificial intelligence is particularly important for the development of entrepreneurship and the creation of new business models. Each of the areas presented could constitute a separate subchapter in the full version of the work, allowing for an in-depth analysis of the specifics of implementations and their consequences. In the trade sector, artificial intelligence plays a key role in personalising offers and managing customer relations. Recommendation algorithms analyse purchase history, consumer preferences, and behavioural data, enabling offers to be tailored to the individual needs of customers (Różanowska, 2007). AI also supports inventory management, demand forecasting, and real-time price optimisation. This enables commercial enterprises to increase sales, reduce losses, and improve customer experience, thereby strengthening their competitive position. The financial sector is one of the most advanced areas in terms of the use of artificial intelligence. AI is used in credit risk analysis, financial fraud detection, customer service automation, and investment portfolio management. Learning algorithms allow for the rapid processing of huge amounts of financial data, which increases the accuracy of assessments and decisions (Stylec-Szromek, 2018). At the same time, the use of AI in finance raises regulatory and ethical challenges related to the transparency of algorithms and the protection of customer data. In industry, artificial intelligence is one of the pillars of the Industry 4.0 concept. AI systems are used to monitor production processes, predictive maintenance, and optimise energy and raw material consumption. By analysing data from sensors and machines, it is possible to detect faults early, which reduces downtime and increases production efficiency. AI also supports product design and flexible adaptation of production to changing market needs. In the area of logistics and transport, artificial intelligence enables route optimisation, fleet management, and forecasting of transport service demand. AI algorithms allow for better supply chain planning, cost reduction, and a reduction in the environmental impact of logistics activities. The development of autonomous vehicles and intelligent warehouse systems further increases the transformative potential of AI in this sector. Healthcare is one of the areas where the use of artificial intelligence can bring significant social benefits. AI is used in medical diagnostics, image analysis, personalisation of therapies, and healthcare system management. Learning algorithms support doctors in making clinical decisions, improving the accuracy of diagnoses, and reducing treatment time. At the same time, the implementation of AI in healthcare requires particular attention to data security and ethical issues. In the education sector, artificial intelligence contributes to the development of personalised forms of education and new teaching models. AI-based systems enable the adaptation of educational content to the individual needs of students, progress monitoring, and automated assessment. AI-supported education promotes the development of digital and entrepreneurial skills, preparing future staff to function in a knowledge-based economy. Marketing is another area where artificial intelligence is used intensively. Algorithms that analyse consumer data enable precise targeting of advertising campaigns, forecasting customer behaviour and optimising marketing communication. AI also enables automatic content generation, sentiment analysis, and customer relationship management in digital channels (Skalfista, Mikelsten, Teigens, 2020). As a result, marketing becomes more effective, measurable, and data-driven. In agriculture, artificial intelligence supports the development of precision farming, enabling the optimisation of natural resource use. Analysis of data from satellites, drones, and sensors allows for monitoring the condition of crops, forecasting yields, and identifying threats such as plant diseases or droughts. The use of AI contributes to increased agricultural productivity and sustainable environmental management. Public administration is also increasingly turning to AI-based solutions. AI supports the automation of administrative procedures, the analysis of public data, and the improvement of the quality of services provided to citizens (Walicka & Czemiel-Grzybowska, 2023). Intelligent systems can streamline decision-making processes, increase the transparency of administrative activities and reduce the operating costs of public institutions. Finally, artificial intelligence is used in creative industries such as media, art, design, and entertainment. Generative algorithms enable the creation of visual, musical, and textual content, supporting the creative process and opening up new business opportunities. However, the use of AI in these sectors raises questions about authorship, the value of creativity, and the relationship between human and algorithmic creativity. In summary, the applications of artificial intelligence in various sectors of the economy demonstrate its versatile and transformative nature. AI not only improves the functioning of existing industries, but also contributes to the emergence of new forms of entrepreneurship and business models (Datsenko, 2024). Sectoral analysis provides a better understanding of the scale and diversity of AI's impact and provides a basis for further reflection on its role in shaping the future of the economy and entrepreneurship.

1.9 THE IMPACT OF ARTIFICIAL INTELLIGENCE ON THE COMPETITIVENESS OF ENTERPRISES

Artificial intelligence is increasingly influencing the mechanisms that shape the competitiveness of enterprises, changing traditional sources of market advantage, and relationships between economic entities. In a data-driven economy, the ability to effectively use AI-based solutions is becoming one of the key factors determining a company's competitive position. Competition is no longer based solely on production costs, product quality, or access to capital, but increasingly on the ability to process information, learn and adapt to a dynamically changing environment. One of the fundamental sources of competitive advantage in the era of artificial intelligence is the ability to collect, integrate, and analyse data. Companies with large and diverse data sets can create more accurate predictive models, better understand customer behaviour, and identify market changes more quickly. As a result, they are able to offer more tailored products and services, manage customer relationships more effectively and optimise their internal processes (Jorzik et al., 2024). Data is no longer just an auxiliary resource, but a strategic asset whose importance grows with its reusability and scalability. Another important factor influencing the competitiveness of companies is the economics of scale associated with the development and training of artificial intelligence models. Large organisations and entities operating within global digital ecosystems have the resources to invest in advanced computing infrastructure, teams of specialists, and long-term model training processes. This results in the accumulation of technological advantages that are difficult for smaller entities to replicate. At the same time, the development of ready-made AI-based tools and services lowers the barriers to entry for new market participants, enabling them to use advanced solutions without incurring high initial costs (Climent et al., 2024). In this context, digital platforms that integrate data, users, and AI-based services play a special role. These platforms are becoming central nodes of competition, shaping the conditions of access to markets and technological resources. Companies operating within them can benefit from network effects, faster scaling of operations, and access to advanced analytical tools. At the same time, the growing role of platforms is leading to changes in the structure of competition, strengthening the position of the largest players and increasing the dependence of smaller companies on external technological ecosystems. The impact of artificial intelligence on the competitiveness of enterprises also raises questions about market competition and the position of small and medium-sized enterprises. On the one hand, AI can promote concentration, enabling the largest players to further strengthen their position thanks to the scale of data and resources. On the other hand, small and medium-sized enterprises can leverage organisational flexibility, niche markets, and specialist knowledge to compete effectively through innovative AI applications (Mhaskey, 2024). Access to cloud-based solutions and tools based on ready-to-use models allows them to implement advanced technologies without having to build their own infrastructure. In summary, artificial intelligence is significantly transforming the competitive landscape, introducing new sources of advantage and changing market dynamics. The competitiveness of enterprises increasingly depends on their ability to manage data, exploit economies of scale and operate within digital platforms and ecosystems. At the same time, the impact of AI on market structure remains ambivalent, creating both opportunities and challenges for entities of various sizes, which makes it an important area for further analysis and research.

1.10 CHALLENGES AND RISKS ASSOCIATED WITH THE USE OF ARTIFICIAL INTELLIGENCE

The dynamic development and increasingly widespread use of artificial intelligence in the economy is associated not only with numerous benefits, but also with a growing number of challenges and risks of a technological, social, ethical, and legal nature. The scale and pace of implementation of AI-based solutions mean that many of these problems only become apparent in practice, often in ways that are difficult to predict. For this reason, the issues of responsible and conscious use of artificial intelligence are becoming one of the key topics of scientific and public debate. One of the fundamental challenges is algorithm ethics, understood as a set of principles for designing and using AI systems in a manner consistent with social values. Algorithms are increasingly involved in decision-making processes that have a real impact on people's lives, such as employee recruitment, credit granting, and risk assessment. This necessitates reflection on the responsibility for decisions made with the support of AI and on the limits of automation in socially sensitive areas. Closely related to this problem is the issue of data bias, or so-called algorithmic bias. AI systems learn from historical data, which may reflect existing inequalities, stereotypes, or errors. As a result, algorithms may unknowingly perpetuate or reinforce discriminatory patterns, even though they formally operate in an "objective" manner. For businesses, this poses reputational and legal risks and the loss of stakeholder trust. Another significant challenge is the lack of transparency of artificial intelligence models, especially those based on deep learning (Hasan, 2025). The complexity of algorithms makes the decision-making process difficult to explain, even for their creators. The limited ability to interpret results makes it difficult to control AI systems and assess their correctness and compliance with applicable standards. This problem is particularly important in regulated sectors such as finance, healthcare, and public administration. Issues related to data security and privacy are no less important. Artificial intelligence relies on the processing of large amounts of information, often of a sensitive nature. Security breaches, data leaks or misuse of information can lead to serious legal and social consequences. Companies must therefore invest in advanced data protection mechanisms and comply with the principles of minimisation and appropriate information management. The development of AI also brings legal and regulatory challenges. The law often lags behind rapid technological progress, leading to uncertainty about responsibility for the actions of AI systems, the protection of user rights and the rules for data use. The lack of consistent regulation can, on the one hand, hamper innovation and, on the other, increase the risk of abuse. Another significant area of risk is the impact of artificial intelligence on the labour market and social inequalities. The automation of tasks is leading to the disappearance of certain professions, while increasing the demand for highly skilled digital competences (Martinez, 2018). This process may exacerbate inequalities between groups of workers, economic sectors, and regions if it is not supported by appropriate educational and social policies.

The table below summarises the main challenges and risks associated with the use of artificial intelligence, along with their potential consequences for businesses:

AREA OF RISK	*NATURE OF THE CHALLENGE*	*POTENTIAL CONSEQUENCES FOR BUSINESSES*
Algorithm ethics	Automation of decisions with high social impact	Loss of trust, social conflicts, reputational risk
Data bias	Inequalities encoded in training data	Discrimination, legal sanctions, erroneous decisions
Transparency of models	Difficulty interpreting how algorithms work	Limited control, audit issues
Security and privacy	Processing of large sets of sensitive data	Data leaks, regulatory penalties
Law and regulations	Regulations not keeping pace with AI developments	Legal uncertainty, implementation barriers
Labour market	Automation and changes in employment structure	Inequalities, skills shortages

In summary, the challenges and risks associated with the development of artificial intelligence are multidimensional and require a systemic approach. Responsible implementation of AI in enterprises should combine innovation with careful consideration, attention to safety, and active management of social impacts. Only such an approach allows the full potential of artificial intelligence to be exploited while minimising its negative consequences.

1.11 ENTREPRENEURIAL SKILLS IN THE ERA OF ARTIFICIAL INTELLIGENCE

The development of artificial intelligence is leading to a significant change in the competency profile of the modern entrepreneur. In a data- and algorithm-driven economy, traditional management skills such as planning, organising, and controlling remain important, but are no longer sufficient for effective market performance. Entrepreneurs in the AI era must combine business knowledge with digital, analytical, and social skills that enable them to effectively exploit the potential of new technologies while taking into account their consequences. One of the key competencies is the ability to understand data and work in an information environment. This is not just about technical knowledge of analytical tools, but about the ability to interpret the results generated by AI systems, critically assess their quality and use data in decision-making processes. Entrepreneurs should be able to formulate the right business questions that can be supported by data analysis and understand the limitations of algorithmic models. Equally important is the ability to work effectively with artificial intelligence systems. In the new model of entrepreneurship, AI does not replace the entrepreneur, but becomes their partner in the decision-making process. This requires the ability to integrate algorithmic recommendations with human experience, intuition, and responsibility (Saija, 2020). Entrepreneurs must be able to supervise the operation of AI systems, identify potential errors and decide on the scope of automation of individual processes. Another important area of competence is managing technological change. The implementation of AI-based solutions involves the reorganisation of processes, changes in employee roles and the need to adapt the organisational culture. Entrepreneurs should be able to communicate the goals of the transformation, build acceptance for change and support the development of employee competencies. Effective leadership in the AI era involves combining a technological vision with sensitivity to the social impact of innovation. Interdisciplinarity is also becoming an important competence. AI-based entrepreneurship operates at the intersection of various fields, such as IT, economics, law, ethics, and social sciences. An entrepreneur does not need to be an expert in each of these fields, but should understand their basic interrelationships and be able to work with teams with diverse competencies. The ability to integrate knowledge from different areas fosters the creation of innovative and responsible solutions. Social responsibility is also an integral part of an entrepreneur's competence in the era of artificial intelligence. Decisions made with the support of AI can affect employees, customers, and entire communities. Entrepreneurs should be aware of the social and ethical consequences of the technologies they implement, ensure transparency in their actions and respect the principles of data protection and equal treatment. A responsible approach to AI development is becoming not only a regulatory requirement, but also an element of building long-term trust and reputation for a company. In summary, the competencies of an entrepreneur in the era of artificial intelligence are multidimensional and dynamic (Cao, 2025). They include the ability to work with data, interact with AI systems, manage change, integrate knowledge, and provide responsible leadership. It is the combination of these competencies that determines the ability of entrepreneurs to function effectively and develop in the new technological paradigm.

1.12 SCENARIOS FOR THE FUTURE OF ENTREPRENEURSHIP IN THE CONTEXT OF ARTIFICIAL INTELLIGENCE DEVELOPMENT

The ongoing integration of artificial intelligence into economic processes makes the future of entrepreneurship increasingly complex and multidimensional. The pace of technological development, the degree of its dissemination, and the response of businesses, public institutions, and society determine the various possible paths of economic evolution. For this reason, the scenario approach is a useful analytical tool for capturing alternative directions for the development of entrepreneurship and the potential consequences of different adaptation strategies towards artificial intelligence. One of the most likely directions of development is the scenario of intensive automation, in which companies focus on maximising the use of artificial intelligence to increase efficiency, reduce costs, and scale up their operations. In this approach, entrepreneurship is based on the design and implementation of automated systems capable of making operational decisions independently. Competitive advantage comes from access to technological infrastructure, data, and the ability to rapidly implement algorithmic innovations. Although this scenario is conducive to productivity growth and economic dynamism, it can also lead to the marginalisation of smaller entities and the intensification of social problems related to the labour market. An alternative path is a scenario of symbiosis between humans and technology, in which artificial intelligence serves as a tool to enhance human competencies rather than replace them. In this view, entrepreneurship develops on the basis of cooperation between entrepreneurs, employees, and AI systems, while maintaining the primacy of humans in areas requiring creativity, empathy, and responsibility. Companies invest in the development of digital competences, build flexible organisational structures and use AI to support innovation, not just to optimise costs. This scenario is conducive to the creation of sustainable business models and the building of long-term social value. There is also the possibility of a crisis scenario, in which the rapid development of artificial intelligence leads to growing social tensions, regulatory problems and a loss of trust in technology. In this scenario, entrepreneurship operates in conditions of growing legal uncertainty, increased regulatory control, and pressure from public opinion. The implementation of innovation may slow down, and entrepreneurs may be forced to focus more on risk management, regulatory compliance, and ethical aspects. Although this scenario may limit the dynamics of development, it also creates space for the formation of more responsible and transparent forms of entrepreneurship. The most groundbreaking variant is the radical innovation scenario, in which artificial intelligence becomes an impetus for fundamental change in economic and social structures. In this scenario, new industries, business models, and forms of entrepreneurship emerge, often transcending existing sectoral boundaries. Entrepreneurs operate in global innovation ecosystems, harnessing the potential of AI to create solutions that redefine the way we work, consume, and create value. This scenario involves a high level of risk and uncertainty, but at the same time offers the greatest potential for growth and economic transformation (Akhil et al.,2023). In practice, the future of entrepreneurship is likely to be shaped by a combination of the scenarios presented, depending on the sectoral, regional, and institutional context. Entrepreneurs will be forced to operate in an environment of coexisting automation, human–technology collaboration, increasing regulatory requirements and disruptive innovation. The ability to respond flexibly to these diverse challenges and the ability to strategically leverage artificial intelligence may prove crucial in shaping the future of entrepreneurship in the coming decades.

1.13 SUMMARY

The analysis of the role of artificial intelligence in the development of modern entrepreneurship presented in this chapter has allowed for a multidimensional approach to this phenomenon, going beyond the technocentric perception of AI as the next stage of automation. The theoretical and analytical approach used, based on an in-depth review of the literature on the subject, analysis of economic and management concepts, and case studies of companies implementing AI-based solutions, has made it possible to analytical approach, based on an in-depth review of the literature on the subject, an analysis of economic and management concepts, and case studies of companies implementing AI-based solutions, has made it possible to present artificial intelligence as a factor of organisational transformation, a driver of product and process innovation, and a potential new paradigm for the development of entrepreneurship. These conclusions confirm the previously proposed research hypotheses, indicating that the impact of AI is not limited to improving operational efficiency, but includes deeper changes in the way value is created, organisational structures and relationships between entrepreneurs, technology, and the market. However, a critical assessment of the research conducted points to a number of significant methodological and cognitive limitations. First, the predominantly qualitative nature of the analyses, based mainly on a review of the literature and secondary data, limits the possibility of empirical verification of the cause-and-effect relationship between the implementation of AI solutions and the economic performance of enterprises. The lack of quantitative research on a representative sample of companies makes it impossible to clearly determine the scale of the impact of artificial intelligence on productivity, innovation, or the sustainability of competitive advantage. Secondly, the case studies presented largely concern companies operating in technologically advanced sectors or those with significant capital and competence resources, which may lead to a selection effect and overrepresentation of "good practices". As a result, the picture of the transformation of enterprises under the influence of AI may be overly optimistic with regard to smaller, less computerised entities or those operating in traditional sectors. Thirdly, the dynamic and rapid development of artificial intelligence technology means that some of the conclusions are temporary in nature and may become obsolete with the emergence of new technological models, legal regulations or changes in the institutional environment. Despite these limitations, the chapter makes an important cognitive contribution by broadening the understanding of entrepreneurship in an algorithmic economy. A novel aspect of the approach is the proposal of a perspective in which artificial intelligence is treated not only as a tool for increasing efficiency, but also as an element that shapes the entrepreneurial process. In particular, it shows a shift from entrepreneurship based on intuition and individual experience to entrepreneurship based on data, predictive models, and human interaction with algorithmic systems. The growing importance of algorithmic and platform entrepreneurship, in which data, digital infrastructure, and the ability to integrate technology within innovation ecosystems are becoming key resources, is also emphasised. These conclusions deepen existing theories of entrepreneurship, pointing to the need for their revision in light of advancing cognitive automation. The significance of the research should be considered not only in theoretical terms, but also in practical and applicational terms. For management and economics sciences, the presented conclusions provide a basis for further research on the long-term effects of AI implementation in enterprises, including its impact on business models, employment structure and value creation mechanisms. For economic practice, the chapter provides arguments for the need for a strategic approach to the implementation of artificial intelligence, covering not only technological investments, but also the development of employee competences, changes in organisational culture and the building of organisational adaptability. It is emphasised that the lack of such an approach may lead to superficial digitalisation that does not fully exploit the transformative potential of AI. Another important aspect of the research is its social and institutional dimension. The chapter points out that the growing importance of artificial intelligence in business raises new challenges in the areas of the labour market, technological inequality, and ethical responsibility for decisions made by algorithmic systems. These conclusions can form the basis for the design of public policies aimed at supporting the responsible adoption of AI, the development of digital skills, and the mitigation of the negative social effects of automation. In particular, the role of the state and public institutions in creating a regulatory framework that promotes innovation while protecting the interests of employees, consumers, and smaller economic entities was emphasised (Cao, 2025). The information obtained in this chapter can be used as a starting point for further empirical research, both quantitative and qualitative, including analysis of sectoral and regional differences and international comparisons. A particularly promising direction for further research seems to be the analysis of the long-term effects of AI implementation on the growth dynamics of enterprises, the sustainability of innovation and changes in the relationship between capital, labour, and technology (Coeckelbergh, 2020).

In addition, the conclusions presented may be used in the design of education programmes in the field of entrepreneurship and management, taking into account competences related to working with data, algorithms, and the ethical dimension of the use of artificial intelligence. In summary, the chapter presents artificial intelligence as a systemic phenomenon that simultaneously transforms the functioning of enterprises, stimulates innovation, and redefines the basic assumptions of entrepreneurship as a theoretical and practical category (Climent et al.,2024). Despite research limitations, the analyses presented provide consistent and in-depth conclusions that can make a valuable contribution to further scientific debate and practical actions for the conscious and responsible use of the potential of artificial intelligence in the development of entrepreneurship.

REFERENCES

Acemoglu, D. (2021). *Harms of AI* (NBER Working Paper No. 29247). National Bureau of Economic Research.

Ai, A. I. (2022). *The fourth industrial revolution*. American Psychological Association.

AI Now Institute. (2017). *AI now 2017 report*.

AI Now Institute. (2018). *AI now report 2018*. New York University.

Ai, W. I. (2018). *Artificial intelligence (AI) in healthcare and research*. Nuffield Council on Bioethics.

Akhil, K., Sanganbhatla, S., & Boddapatl, B. (2023). Cognitive science: Towards a multi-disciplinary sense for solving a complex mechanism. In: *Proceedings of the 5th International Conference on Advances in Computing, Communication Control and Networking (ICAC3N)* (pp. 1221–1227). IEEE.

Beraja, M., Yang, D. Y., & Yuchtman, N. (2023). AI-tocracy. *The Quarterly Journal of Economics*, *138*(3), 1349–1402.

Bielińska-Dusza, E. (2022). Technological transformation of enterprises as a result of the application of artificial intelligence. *Organisation and Management, 191*(2), 189–208.

Bortnowska, H., et al. (2024). The use of artificial intelligence applications in learning – a report on a survey of secondary school students. *School–Profession–Work, 28*, 89–110.

Campolo, A., Sanfilippo, M., Whittaker, M., & Crawford, K. (2017). *AI Now 2017 report*. AI Now Institute.

Cao, L. (2025). Trans-AI/DS: Transformative, transdisciplinary and translational artificial intelligence and data science. *International Journal of Data Science and Analytics, 20*(2), 1617–1629.

Climent, R. C., Haftor, D. M., & Staniewski, M. W. (2024). AI-enabled business models for competitive advantage. *Journal of Innovation & Knowledge, 9*(3), 100532.

Coeckelbergh, M. (2020). *AI ethics*. MIT Press.

D'Alfonso, S. (2020). AI in mental health. *Current Opinion in Psychology*, *36*, 112–117.

Datsenko, Y. (2024). Shaping mechanisms for implementing artificial intelligence technologies in a company's personnel management system.

Furman, J., & Seamans, R. (2019). AI and the economy. *Innovation Policy and the Economy*, *19*(1), 161–191.

Grace, K., et al. (2025). Thousands of AI authors on the future of AI. *Journal of Artificial Intelligence Research*, *84*, 1–40.

Hasan, M. M. (2025). Federated learning models for privacy-preserving AI in enterprise decision systems. *International Journal of Business and Economics Insights*, *5*(3), 238–269.

Johnson, D. G., & Verdicchio, M. (2017). AI anxiety. *Journal of the Association for Information Science and Technology*, *68*(9), 2267–2270.

Jorzik, P., Klein, S. P., Kanbach, D. K., & Kraus, S. (2024). AI-driven business model innovation: A systematic review and research agenda. *Journal of Business Research*, *182*, 114764.

Kleiber, M. (2024). Uncontrolled development of AI is a problem for humanity. *Science Quarterly, 2*.

Kłoczko, A. (2024). The use of artificial intelligence in organisational management as a potential for cost reduction. *Scientific Journals of the Częstochowa University of Technology. Management*, *55*(1), 61–77.

Konopka, M. N. (2023). Everyone knows about AI. A review of Polish public opinion on artificial intelligence. *Press Studies Journal*, *4*(256), 127–142.

Kuang, Y., et al. (2014). Double stimulations during the follicular and luteal phases of poor responders in IVF/ICSI programmes (Shanghai protocol). *Reproductive Biomedicine Online*, *29*(6), 684–691.

Kuang, Y., et al. (2014). Luteal-phase ovarian stimulation is feasible for producing competent oocytes in women undergoing IVF/ICSI. *Fertility and Sterility*, *101*(1), 105–111.

Kuang, Y., et al. (2015). Medroxyprogesterone acetate is an effective oral alternative for preventing premature LH surges. *Fertility and Sterility*, *104*(1), 62–70.

Martinez, R. (2018). Artificial intelligence: Distinguishing between types & definitions. *Nevada Law Journal*, *19*, 1015–1042.

Mhaskey, S. V. (2024). Integration of AI in ERP systems: Opportunities, challenges, and implications. *International Journal of Computer Engineering in Research Trends*, *11*(12), 1–9.

Millington, I. (2019). *AI for games* (3rd ed.). CRC Press.

Ng, D. T. K., et al. (2023). A review of AI teaching and learning from 2000 to 2020. *Education and Information Technologies*, *28*(7), 8445–8501.

Panigutti, C., et al. (2023). The role of explainable AI in the context of the AI Act. In *Proceedings of the ACM Conference on Fairness, Accountability, and Transparency*.

Passi, S., & Vorvoreanu, M. (2022). Overreliance on AI literature review. *Microsoft Research*.

Ransbotham, S., et al. (2019). *Winning with AI*. MIT Sloan Management Review.

Różanowski, K. (2007). Artificial intelligence: Development, opportunities and threats. *Scientific Journals of the Warsaw University of Information Technology*, *2*(2), 109–135.

Sajja, P. S. (2020). Introduction to artificial intelligence. In *Illustrated computational intelligence* (pp. 1–25). Springer.

Schank, R. C. (1991). Where's the AI? *AI Magazine*, *12*(4), 38.

Skalfist, P., Mikelsten, D., & Teigens, V. (2020). *Artificial intelligence: The fourth industrial revolution*. Cambridge Stanford Books.

Stylec-Szromek, P. (2018). Artificial intelligence – law, responsibility, ethics. *Scientific Journals of the Silesian University of Technology. Organisation and Management*.

Walicka, M., & Czemiel-Grzybowska, W. (2023). Artificial intelligence in enterprise capital management in the era of Industry 5.0. *Management Academy*.

Weinert, A. (2024). AI in strategic management – the example of the Localo tool. In: Chodyka, M. (ed) *Society–Technology–Economy* (pp. 59–67).

Whittaker, M., et al. (2018). *AI Now report 2018*. AI Now Institute.

Yu, S., et al. (2018). New application of dydrogesterone as part of progestin-primed ovarian stimulation protocol. *Human Reproduction, 33*(2), 229–237.

2

Integrated AI Systems Supporting Strategic, Operational, and Financial Management

An Overview of Approaches and Case Studies

2.1 INTRODUCTION

The contemporary business arena is constantly shaped by the forces of a dynamic and unpredictable environment, aptly described by the acronym VUCA (Volatility, Uncertainty, Complexity, Ambiguity; Bennett & Lemoine, 2014). Market globalisation, rapid technological progress, and rapidly changing

DOI:10.1201/9781042024131-3

legal regulations and consumer expectations mean that traditional, linear management methods and decision-making processes based on historical data are becoming less effective. Effective and efficient management now requires not only the rapid processing of massive, diverse data sets (Big Data) in real time, but above all the ability to predictively model the future and ensure strategic consistency at all organisational levels (Chen et al., 2023).

In this highly demanding landscape, Artificial Intelligence (AI) technologies – including Machine Learning (ML), Deep Learning (DL), and Natural Language Processing (NLP) – are emerging as a key enabler for transforming decision-making processes from reactive to proactive (Davenport & Ronanki, 2018). AI offers the ability to identify patterns invisible to humans, make accurate predictions, and recommend optimal courses of action, which can lead to a significant improvement in the quality of strategic, operational, and financial decisions within a company (Raisch & Krakowski, 2021).

However, a key innovative direction is the development and implementation of Integrated AI Systems (IASI). ISAI go beyond single, isolated applications (often operating in organisational silos) to create a coherent, corporate architecture that integrates AI analyses and recommendations to support three fundamental levels of management: strategic, operational, and financial. This integration requires a unified data architecture and a Single Source of Truth (SSOT) concept that ensures consistency, quality and real-time data availability for all analytical and decision-making modules (Batini et al., 2022; Chen et al., 2023).

The literature emphasises that effective enterprise-wide AI implementation requires a holistic approach to system architecture design, data infrastructure, and management processes, rather than simply implementing individual models or analytical tools (Batini et al., 2022). Integrated AI systems enable knowledge sharing between different organisational functions, eliminate conflicting decision recommendations and achieve synergistic effects, which directly translates into improved key performance indicators (KPIs).

At the same time, the issue of explainability of AI models (Explainable Artificial Intelligence – XAI) remains a significant challenge, especially at the level of strategic and financial decisions, where transparency, trust, and the ability to audit algorithmic recommendations play a key role (Guidotti et al., 2019). A lack of adequate explainability may limit the acceptance of AI systems by management, even in situations where the models are highly predictive.

Therefore, understanding the mechanisms, benefits and limitations of full AI integration in an enterprise is an important area of research and management practice. This chapter focuses on analysing the theoretical foundations of Integrated AI Systems, their architecture and the role of a single data source, as well as assessing the impact of these systems on decision-making processes and organisational effectiveness. The following sections of the paper present a review of the literature, the research methodology used, an analysis of case studies, and a discussion of the results in the context of future directions for the development of ISA.

2.2 METHODS

The dynamic development of artificial intelligence technology and the growing complexity of decision-making processes in organisations mean that increasing attention is being paid to the integration of AI systems across the entire enterprise (Davenport & Ronanki, 2018; Raisch & Krakowski, 2021). Previous research indicates that although isolated AI implementations bring measurable operational benefits, their strategic potential remains limited in the absence of a coherent data architecture and cross-functional integration (Batini et al., 2022; Chen et al., 2023). Consequently, it is justified to undertake research focusing on the analysis of synergistic effects resulting from the full integration of AI systems, the role of a unified data architecture, and the importance of the explainability of AI models in top-level decision-making processes (Guidotti et al., 2019).

The main objective of this paper is to conduct a critical and systematic analysis of the theoretical foundations and practical implementations of Integrated Artificial Intelligence Systems (IAIS) in three key areas of business management: strategic, operational, and financial. Achieving this objective requires both the systematisation of existing theoretical knowledge and the analysis of empirical examples of integrated AI solutions.

As part of the main objective, specific objectives have been formulated, including the systematisation of knowledge on ISAI architecture and the role of a single source of truth (SSOT), the identification of key AI methods and algorithms, such as reinforcement learning and time series models, used in decision-making processes at various levels of management, assessing the impact of full AI integration on key business performance indicators (KPIs), empirically analysing the transformative potential of ZSAI based on case studies, and identifying the main implementation barriers, with particular emphasis on the issue of Explainable Artificial Intelligence (XAI).

Based on a review of the literature and the research objectives formulated, the following research hypotheses were proposed:

Hypothesis H1: An Integrated AI System (IASS) provides significantly higher synergistic benefits, measured by an increase in return on investment (ROI) and operational efficiency, compared to the sum of the benefits of isolated AI implementations in the areas of strategic, operational, and financial management (Davenport & Ronanki, 2018; Raisch & Krakowski, 2021).

Hypothesis H2: The effectiveness of an Integrated AI System is directly dependent on the existence of a single corporate data platform (Single Source of Truth – SSOT), which ensures consistency, high quality, and real-time data availability for all AI modules (Batini et al., 2022; Chen et al., 2023).

Hypothesis H3: The lack of an adequate level of explainability of AI models (XAI) at the strategic and financial level is a significant barrier to the acceptance and effective use of Integrated AI Systems in top-level decision-making processes, regardless of the predictive accuracy of the models (Guidotti et al., 2019; Raisch & Krakowski, 2021).

The hypotheses were verified using a comparative analysis of case studies, including both an assessment of changes in selected business performance indicators and a qualitative analysis of decision-making processes supported by Integrated AI Systems. The research approach used allows for the identification of relationships between the degree of AI system integration, data architecture, and the level of model explainability, and actual organisational and financial effects.

The results of the empirical analysis provide a basis for assessing the validity of the hypotheses and for drawing conclusions about the effectiveness of ZSAI as a tool supporting strategic, operational, and financial management. The following sections of the chapter present a detailed analysis of the cases, the results of the research and their interpretation in the context of existing theories of management and artificial intelligence.

2.3 THEORETICAL FOUNDATIONS

The Integrated AI System (IASI) represents an evolutionary stage of development beyond classical business informatics, functioning as a highly complex and coherent analytical and decision-making platform (Dean et al., 1995). What is artificial intelligence? Its primary goal is to transform heterogeneous and large-scale data sets into coherent, measurable, and proactive business decisions (Prasanth et al., 2023). The unique value of ZSAI stems from the deliberate and deep integration of various sub-disciplines of artificial intelligence, such as machine learning (ML), deep learning (DL), natural language processing (NLP), and computer vision, and then directly linking them to critical corporate systems operating within the organisation, including ERP (Enterprise Resource Planning), CRM (Customer Relationship Management), and Business Intelligence (BI) systems (McCarthy, 2007).

Integration understood in this way not only enables the immediate flow of information between analytical and operational layers, but also ensures that the recommendations generated by AI algorithms are operationally feasible and economically justified. The ZSAI architecture is modular and layered, which promotes the scalability of the solution and its continuous adaptation to changing conditions and business needs.

There are three main interdependent components in the ZSAI structure. The first is the Data Ingestion Layer, which acts as a gateway for all data streams (Erraissi & Belangour, 2018). Its task is to acquire, standardise, and aggregate large volumes of both structured data from transactional and financial systems and unstructured data, including text, images, and sensory data generated by Internet of Things (IoT) systems (Murarka et al., 2024). This data can come from both internal and external sources, such as market data or social media.

The second component, which serves as the analytical core of the system, is the Data Processing and Modelling Layer. In this environment, typically based on Big Data architectures (e.g., data lakes) and scalable cloud infrastructure, data undergoes cleaning, validation, and transformation processes (Zhu et al., 2019). It is then used to train advanced AI/ML models. The selection of algorithms is determined by the specifics of the problem being solved and may include, among others, neural networks in time series forecasting, decision trees in risk analysis, or reinforcement learning methods in the optimisation of dynamic processes (Thomas et al., 2016; Wiering et al., 2012; Shakya et al., 2023).

The third key component is the Decision Layer, whose task is to provide predictions and recommendations to end users and to control executive systems via interfaces and Application Programming Interfaces (APIs). An important element of this layer is the implementation of a feedback loop, in which the results of decisions made are automatically used to recalibrate models and further train the system (adaptive learning), enabling continuous improvement in the precision and accuracy of the recommendations generated.

The theoretical justification for the functioning of ZSAI is the pursuit of data synergy and the elimination of local optimisation. Local optimisation, characteristic of organisations using fragmented and uncoordinated information systems, leads to situations where improvements in one area come at the expense of the overall efficiency of the enterprise (Nambiar & Mundra, 2022). In ZSAI, decisions made at the operational level must be consistent with long-term strategic goals and demonstrate a measurable, positive financial impact (Pisoni et al., 2021). This problem is solved by using a common, integrated enterprise data model.

This model enables the integration of data in terms of time and space, so that, for example, demand prediction models supporting strategic decisions can directly feed into inventory planning systems at the operational level, which in turn improves the accuracy of financial forecasts. Achieving such decision-making consistency is based on two key theoretical pillars.

The first is the concept of a Single Source of Truth (SSOT), understood as a technical and organisational condition ensuring that all system modules and all organisational units operate on the same, verified, and up-to-date data (Zhang et al., 2021). SSOT is a prerequisite for eliminating errors resulting from input data inconsistencies.

The second pillar consists of corporate ontologies and taxonomies, which are formal descriptions of concepts, relationships, and processes functioning in a given business ecosystem. Their application enables different AI modules, operating on different types of data, to interpret complex organisational processes and the relationships between strategic, operational, and financial metrics in a uniform and contextual manner. Ontologies transform data into context-embedded information, which is a sufficient condition for intelligent decision-making (Kusztina et al., 2007).

Data synergy and the establishment of a Single Version of Truth Index therefore constitute the theoretical foundation on which the value of Integrated AI Systems is built. However, translating the analytical potential of these systems into a sustainable competitive advantage requires an understanding of how integrated AI recommendations are adapted and used at different decision-making levels within an organisation. The type of decision and its time horizon determine both the type of AI model used and the scope of data to be processed.

The functioning of ZSAI can be analysed at multiple levels, including strategic, operational, and financial dimensions. This perspective allows for the identification of the diverse information needs of decision-makers, different planning horizons, and the specifics of management processes that determine the selection of artificial intelligence methods (Ratajczak, 2025). In this context, the system architecture is designed as an adaptive structure in which the configuration of analytical models remains a function of the type of decisions supported (Table 2.1).

At the strategic level, ZSAI supports processes of shaping long-term directions for the organisation's development, usually over a three- to five-year period. The dominant tasks here are related to scenario analysis, forecasting market dynamics, and assessing macroeconomic and structural risks. This requires the use of methods capable of processing large, heterogeneous data sets and identifying poorly structured dependencies (Talaat et al., 2024). Particular importance is attached to deep learning models, natural language processing techniques used, among other things, in market sentiment analysis, as well as agent-based simulations that allow the study of the emergent effects of interactions between economic entities. The results obtained form the basis

TABLE 2.1 Applications of artificial intelligence methods in ZSAI by management level

MANAGEMENT LEVEL	*TIME HORIZON*	*MAIN AI FUNCTIONALITIES*	*AI METHODS*
Strategic	Long-term (3–5 years)	Scenario analysis, market forecasting, macroeconomic risk assessment	ML (Deep Learning Networks), NLP (sentiment analysis), Agent simulations
Operational	Short-term (day–month)	Process optimisation, Predictive maintenance, Schedule planning	ML (Classification, Regression), Reinforcement Learning (RL), Computer Vision
Financial	Medium-Long Term	Fraud detection, Credit risk modelling, Automatic budgeting	ML (Anomaly Detection), Time Series Analysis, Logistic Regression

Source: Own study.

for reducing decision uncertainty and support the process of resource allocation in the long term (Pai et al., 2022).

In operational terms, the applications of ZSAI focus on the short-term optimisation of processes, covering a horizon of one day to several months. The priority is to increase the efficiency of resource utilisation, the stability of operations and the ability to respond to disruptions. This layer is dominated by classification and regression algorithms, predictive models used in maintenance, and reinforcement learning methods that enable dynamic adaptation of decisions to changing environmental conditions (Zohuri et al., 2022). In industrial applications, computer vision also plays an important role, supporting the automation of quality control and infrastructure monitoring. The integration of these tools leads to measurable improvements in productivity and reduced operational risk.

At the financial level, ZSAI focuses on strengthening the economic stability of the organisation by improving control and forecasting mechanisms. The processes of fraud detection, credit risk estimation and budget planning support are of key importance. To this end, anomaly detection methods, time series analysis, and logistic regression models are used to quantify the probability of adverse events. The implementation of these solutions contributes to increased transparency of financial processes, improved accuracy of forecasts, and rationalisation of investment decisions (Rane et al., 2024).

The presented approach indicates that AI should be viewed as an integrated, modular analytical environment in which the selection of computational techniques is subordinated to management logic and the level of decision aggregation. The flexibility of the architecture is a prerequisite for the effective transfer of value generated by artificial intelligence models to organisational results. This means that the system's ability to perform diverse decision-making functions does not result solely from the quality of the algorithms used, but also from the principles of its internal organisation, the manner of component integration, and the rules of data and information flow. Consequently, a full understanding of the system's operating mechanisms requires reference to its structural design. This perspective provides a direct starting point for characterising the layered architecture of ZSAI (Figure 2.1).

The architecture of the Integrated AI System is based on a layered functional model that ensures consistency of data processing, continuity of system learning, and integration of decisions made at different levels of management. Figure 2.1 illustrates the layered architecture of the ZSAI, in which the central element is a decision-making and analytical loop based on the concept of a single data source and feedback mechanisms.

The core of the system consists of four interdependent functional layers that form an internal operational loop. The data layer acts as a central information repository and is directly linked to the concept of a Single Source of Truth (SSOT). It ensures the integration, cleaning, standardisation, and sharing of data in a way that guarantees its semantic and temporal consistency throughout the system. SSOT eliminates the risk of inconsistent data interpretation

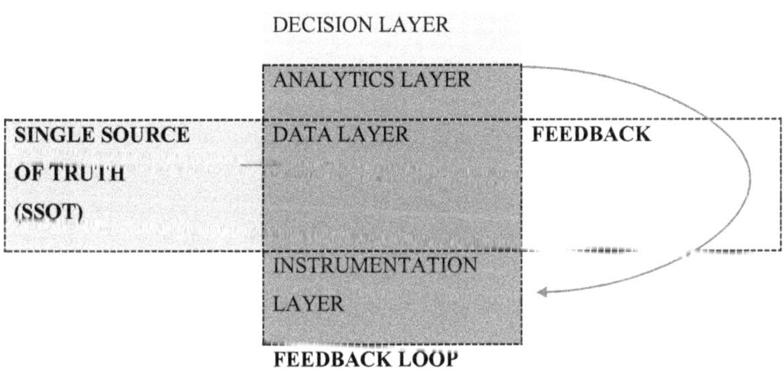

FIGURE 2.1 Layered architecture of the Integrated AI System with a feedback mechanism.

Source: Own work.

between analytical and decision-making modules, which is a prerequisite for the functioning of ZSAI as an integrated system.

On this basis, the analytical layer functions, in which data is transformed into decision-making information through advanced analytics, predictive modelling, data exploration, and visualisation of results. This layer is the environment for the implementation of AI/ML algorithms, whose task is to identify patterns, relationships, and risks relevant to organisational objectives.

The instrumentation layer is responsible for measuring the effects of implemented decisions and operational activities. It includes mechanisms for monitoring, experimentation (e.g., A/B testing), sensory data collection, and performance indicator recording. The data generated in this layer is continuously fed back to the analytical layer, enabling dynamic assessment of decision effectiveness and adaptive tuning of AI models.

The entire internal loop is initiated and closed by the decision layer, which is located outside the operational core of the system. This layer is responsible for formulating objectives, defining decision hypotheses, and interpreting the results provided by the system. Feedback, which is the final element of the cycle, enables the correction of decision-making assumptions and the start of another, improved decision-making cycle, which makes ZSAI a learning system in the organisational sense. However, this mechanism is not limited to a single decision-making act, but extends to the entire management structure, determining how its individual levels interact.

Figure 2.2 shows how the ZSAI architecture supports synergistic decision-making at three key management levels: strategic, operational, and financial. This model illustrates the dynamic, cyclical flow of information and recommendations, in which each level performs a separate function but remains closely linked to the others (Figure 2.2).

At the strategic management level, the ZSAI system supports long-term decision-making by analysing complex market, macroeconomic, and competitive data. Advanced deep learning models and natural language processing techniques are used here to analyse scenarios and forecast trends. The results of these analyses define the directions of action for the operational level.

Operational management focuses on the ongoing implementation of the strategy through process optimisation, resource scheduling and real-time response to changes. Reinforcement learning plays a key role here, enabling dynamic adjustment of operational decisions based on current data and the results of previous actions. Operational results also serve as input for financial management.

The analysis confirms that the Integrated AI System is not only a tool supporting selected business functions, but also the fundamental

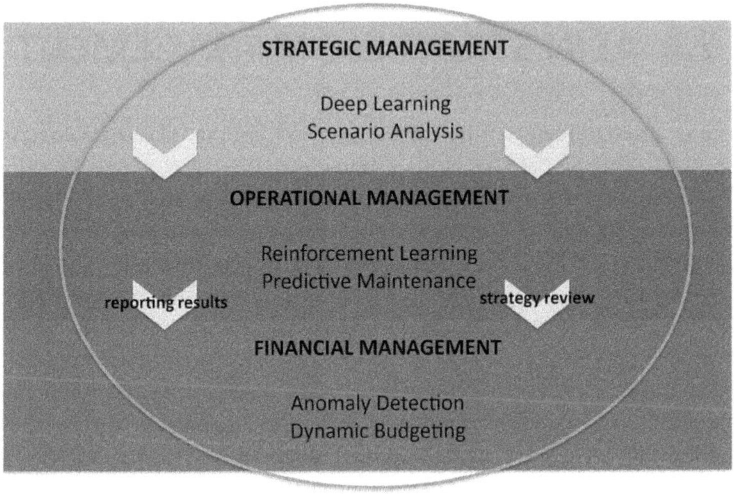

FIGURE 2.2 Application of artificial intelligence methods at management levels in ZSAI.

Source: Own study.

decision-making infrastructure of the organisation. The integration of data, analytics, instrumentation, and management layers within a coherent feedback loop creates an environment in which the knowledge generated by algorithms becomes a direct factor shaping operational activities, strategic directions, and financial results.

A key feature of such a system is its ability to simultaneously ensure information consistency, model adaptability, and consistency of decisions made at different levels of the management structure. Moving away from fragmented, siloed solutions in favour of a unified architecture based on a common data model eliminates local optimisations and shifts the focus of management to the level of the entire organisation. In this sense, ZSAI becomes a mechanism that transforms data into coordinated action, and artificial intelligence ceases to be a technological add-on, taking on the role of a systemic integrator of business processes.

Ultimately, the value of ZSAI materialises in the organisation's ability to make faster, more accurate decisions based on a comprehensive picture of the situation. Thus, the system architecture not only supports management, but redefines its paradigm – from a reactive model to a predictive, learning model that is permanently focused on optimising results across the entire enterprise.

2.4 AI IN STRATEGIC MANAGEMENT

Strategic management is the foundation of an organisation's long-term success, focusing on the formulation, implementation, and evaluation of plans aimed at building a sustainable competitive advantage (Keding, 2021). In an increasingly dynamic and complex economic environment, artificial intelligence systems provide a set of tools that enable a fundamental change in the decision-making paradigm – from reacting to uncertainty to systematically quantifying it and transforming it into manageable risk and identifiable development opportunities.

Traditional forecasting approaches, based mainly on extrapolation of historical time series, prove insufficient in the face of rapid and non-linear market, technological and geopolitical changes. Integrated AI systems address these limitations by using advanced predictive models based on deep learning, in particular neural network architectures capable of simultaneously processing multidimensional and heterogeneous data sets. These models integrate not only internal data, such as sales and operational information, but also external and unstructured sources, including macroeconomic indicators, political decisions, exchange rate volatility and consumer sentiment identified in social media. The transformation of such data into useful analytical measures is possible thanks to the use of natural language processing methods that enable the extraction of knowledge from industry reports, legal regulations, and media content (Alhyasat et al., 2025).

Probabilistic simulations, including the Monte Carlo approach, fed by probability distributions estimated by deep learning models, are an important tool for supporting decision-making in conditions of high uncertainty. This enables managers to assess a wide range of potential market development scenarios and precisely determine their impact on the long-term competitive position and financial condition of the company (Niemiro, 2013). As a result, the strategic planning process is enriched with forward-looking knowledge based on quantitative risk assessment.

Artificial intelligence also plays a key role in improving capital allocation and investment decision-making processes, particularly in the area of mergers and acquisitions. Natural language processing algorithms significantly streamline due diligence procedures by enabling the automatic analysis of extensive legal, financial, and operational documentation. This allows for the identification of potential liabilities, regulatory risks, and areas of synergy that might go unnoticed using traditional analytical methods (Olan et al., 2022).

For internal investments, such as research and development projects or infrastructure development, predictive models enable more accurate estimates of the probability of success and expected rate of return. The analysis covers a wide range of dynamic factors, including the pace of technology commercialisation, market acceptance and cost volatility, which facilitates the optimisation of decisions from the perspective of the entire project portfolio rather than individual initiatives (Prasad et al., 2024).

Contemporary competitive conditions require organisational strategies to be adaptive. ZSAI enables the implementation of the concept of dynamic strategic portfolio management through continuous monitoring of key performance indicators and automatic identification of deviations resulting from changes in the environment. Reinforcement learning mechanisms play a special role here, generating recommendations for alternative courses of action by analysing the consequences of previous actions. These solutions can support decisions regarding the reallocation of financial, marketing, or operational resources between market segments with varying growth potential.

As a result, strategy revision ceases to be a periodic event and becomes a continuous process, based on current data and ongoing assessment of the effectiveness of actions. The integration of the mechanisms described above helps to maintain consistency between the long-term vision of development and the operational implementation of objectives, strengthening the organisation's ability to build a sustainable competitive advantage.

2.4.1 Scenario Analysis, Forecasting, and Investment Decision Support

The effectiveness of strategic management is largely determined by an organisation's ability to anticipate future development conditions and allocate resources rationally in conditions of uncertainty. Forecasting market and technological trends, identifying potential threats, and selecting investment directions are at the core of decision-making processes that determine the sustainability of a company's competitive advantage (Oleś-Filiks, 2025). However, the current scale of data complexity and the pace of change in the environment mean that traditional analytical tools are proving insufficient, which opens up space for the application of advanced artificial intelligence methods within Integrated AI Systems.

Traditional forecasting methods, based primarily on the extrapolation of historical time series, prove insufficient in conditions of rapid and non-linear market, technological and geopolitical changes. ZSAI overcomes these limitations by using advanced predictive models that employ deep learning techniques, in particular neural network architectures capable of processing multidimensional and heterogeneous data sets.

These models integrate both internal data, including sales and operational information, and external sources, often of an unstructured nature. These include macroeconomic indicators, political decisions, exchange rate volatility and consumer sentiment identified in social media. The transformation of this content into measurable analytical parameters is possible thanks to the use of natural language processing methods, which enable the extraction of knowledge from industry reports, legal regulations, and media reports.

Probabilistic simulations, in particular the Monte Carlo approach, fed by probability distributions estimated by AI models, play a key role in strategic planning. This makes it possible to assess a wide range of potential scenarios and determine their impact on the future competitive position and financial condition of the company. As a result, the strategic management process is expanded to include the ability to systematically compare alternative scenarios and quantitatively assess risk.

The knowledge generated by these analyses is directly applicable to capital allocation and investment decision-making processes. Artificial intelligence significantly increases the accuracy of assessments by integrating multiple data categories and identifying relationships that are not visible in traditional financial models. This is particularly important in the area of mergers and acquisitions, where natural language processing algorithms streamline due diligence procedures by enabling the automatic analysis of extensive legal, financial, and operational documentation (Bedekar et al., 2024). This allows for the identification of hidden liabilities, regulatory risks, and potential synergies.

With regard to internal investments, such as research and development projects or infrastructure projects, predictive models enable more accurate estimates of the probability of success and the expected rate of return. The analysis covers a wide range of dynamic factors, including the pace of technology commercialisation, market acceptance, and cost volatility. This allows investment decisions to be optimised across the entire corporate portfolio, rather than just individual projects.

ZSAI thus promotes a transition from an intuitive and fragmented investment assessment model to an approach based on systematic, quantitative risk analysis, and the long-term consequences of decisions. The integration of forecasting, simulation, and capital efficiency assessment mechanisms strengthens an organisation's ability to consciously shape its future competitive position.

2.5 AI IN OPERATIONAL MANAGEMENT

Operational management is a key dimension of a company's functioning, encompassing the processes of transforming material, capital, and human resources into products and services delivered to end users. In the context of digital transformation and advancing automation, artificial intelligence is becoming one of the main factors determining the effectiveness of this area. Its application is primarily focused on increasing process efficiency, reducing operating costs, and improving the quality of activities.

The implementation of AI leads to the creation of a model of intelligent operations, characterised by high flexibility, the ability to predict events, and the precise adaptation of decisions to current conditions. The scope of applications covers several fundamental pillars of operational activity (Wierzbicki & Zaskórski, 2025).

In the area of supply chain optimisation, machine learning methods enable the analysis of extensive historical data sets, market information, and external factors such as weather conditions and transport disruptions. This allows for a significant increase in the accuracy of demand forecasts, which helps to reduce both excessive storage and the risk of product shortages. In addition, AI algorithms support dynamic planning of logistics routes and delivery schedules, leading to shorter order fulfilment times and lower transport costs (Mroczko, 2024).

Predictive maintenance is also an important area of application. By integrating data from Internet of Things sensors that monitor equipment operating parameters, it is possible to detect the symptoms of potential failures at an early stage. Analytical models identify patterns that indicate an increased likelihood of damage, enabling maintenance activities to be planned at the most advantageous time. As a result, the number of unplanned downtimes is reduced, while the life cycle of the technical infrastructure is extended (Korbiel et al., 2024).

In terms of quality control and production organisation, vision systems using image recognition techniques are of particular importance. Automation of the inspection process allows for quick and repeatable detection of defects, minimising subjectivity in assessment, and increasing the stability of quality standards. At the same time, advanced optimisation models enable the creation of production schedules that take into account numerous constraints, such as raw material availability, machine throughput, and order delivery dates (Andrianandrianina Johanesa et al., 2024). This promotes more efficient resource allocation and increases the organisation's ability to respond to disruptions.

As a result, the use of AI leads to a transition from a reactive operational management model to a predictive and adaptive model. Decisions are made based on current data and the projected effects of actions, which translates into improved productivity, process stability, and organisational resilience to risk. Thus, artificial intelligence becomes an integral part of a company's operational infrastructure, supporting the achievement of strategic goals by improving day-to-day operations.

2.5.1 Supply Chain Optimisation

Artificial intelligence is significantly transforming the way modern supply chains operate, enabling a shift from a reactive model to a predictive and adaptive approach. The integration of AI methods into logistics processes promotes greater transparency of flows, reduces uncertainty, and enables more efficient use of resources across the entire organisation (Min, 2010). As a result, operational management gains the ability to identify disruptions earlier and take action to minimise their economic impact.

One of the key areas of application remains demand forecasting. Machine learning models enable the analysis of multidimensional data sets that go beyond traditional historical information. Both logistics and sales data are taken into account, as well as external factors such as weather conditions, macroeconomic changes, and market events. In addition, the use of natural language processing techniques allows for the analysis of consumer sentiment and the identification of early signals of demand changes. Increased forecast accuracy provides the basis for rational inventory management, reducing storage costs and the risk of product obsolescence, while minimising the likelihood of lost sales due to shortages (Nguyen, 2023; Verma, 2024).

Another important area of development is the optimisation of logistics processes in real time. To this end, reinforcement learning algorithms are used, among other things, to enable systems to make decisions in a dynamically changing operating environment. These models take into account a number of variables, such as traffic intensity, transport fleet availability, storage constraints, and fuel cost volatility. This allows for the ongoing reconfiguration of transport plans and effective response to disruptions, including delivery delays and sudden increases in orders.

At the same time, artificial intelligence is widely used in the area of maintenance, especially in the context of predictive maintenance (Kozłowska, 2024). Data generated by Internet of Things sensors enables continuous monitoring of equipment operating parameters such as temperature, vibration, pressure, and energy consumption. Based on this, machine learning models identify patterns that indicate an increased likelihood of failure. Early detection of irregularities allows for the planning of maintenance activities in a way that minimises production disruptions and rationalises the use of technical and human resources.

The application of these solutions leads to a significant reduction in the number of unplanned downtimes, more efficient management of spare parts inventory and an extension of the infrastructure's life cycle. As a result, maintenance ceases to be solely a reactive function and becomes part of the strategic management of operational process reliability.

2.5.2 Intelligent Process Automation (IPA): The Synergy of AI, RPA, and BPM

The integration of artificial intelligence with Robotic Process Automation solutions and the concept of business process management has led to the development of a paradigm known as Intelligent Process Automation. This approach goes beyond the traditional understanding of automation, which is limited to performing repetitive tasks according to predefined rules (Ribeiro et al., 2021). The inclusion of AI components enables systems to interpret data, understand the operational context, and make decisions in situations that previously required human involvement.

One of the most visible areas of transformation is the automation of document circulation in administrative back-office processes. The use of natural language processing methods and image recognition techniques, supported by optical character recognition tools, allows unstructured documents to be converted into data that can be further processed by the system (Rut & Ostafil, 2020). Algorithms identify the required fields, classify document types, and interpret legal and financial records, then transfer the information directly to transaction systems. As a result, operation times are shortened, errors are reduced, and regulatory compliance is improved.

At the same time, intelligent automation is changing the nature of customer interactions. Conversational systems based on language models take over a significant portion of routine queries, ensuring immediate response and consistent service quality. Thanks to learning mechanisms, the accuracy of interpreting user intentions is improved, which translates into greater operational efficiency and the ability for staff to focus on tasks requiring expert competence.

However, a full understanding of the potential of Intelligent Process Automation (IPA) requires an analysis of the relationship between the three pillars of technology that make up this environment. RPA is responsible for the execution layer, performing tasks in IT systems according to specified procedures. It ensures speed, repeatability, and ease of scaling, but lacks interpretative capabilities. This function is taken over by artificial intelligence, which enables data classification, result forecasting, anomaly identification, and decision-making recommendations. Business Process Management (BPM) acts as an orchestrating mechanism, defining the process flow, control points, responsibilities, and performance metrics (Klun & Trkman, 2018).

The synergy of these components lies in their functional complementarity. AI provides knowledge and indicates optimal actions, BPM embeds these decisions in the organisational structure of the process, and RPA ensures their operational execution. This architecture enables the implementation of processes in a comprehensive manner, covering analysis, decision-making, and implementation, while maintaining transparency and auditability.

As a result, organisations move from automating individual tasks to automating entire value streams. Operating costs are reduced, execution times are shortened, and the quality of data and decisions is systematically improved thanks to learning mechanisms. IPA thus strengthens the company's ability to adapt, increasing its efficiency and resilience to changes in the environment.

2.5.3 Human Resource Management (HR)

Artificial intelligence is fundamentally transforming the functioning of human resource management, shifting its focus from administrative activities to a data-driven model. HR is no longer solely an operational support function, but is becoming a participant in strategic processes where decisions on recruitment, skills development, and talent retention are based on systematic interpretation of information. As a result, human capital is managed in a measurable, comparable, and predictable way.

One of the key areas of AI application is the identification of employee turnover risk. Machine learning models analyse a wide range of variables, including employment history, salary dynamics, periodic assessment results, training activity, and absence patterns. Qualitative data, such as satisfaction survey results or teamwork characteristics, are also increasingly being taken into account (Eubanks, 2025). On this basis, the systems identify individuals with an increased likelihood of leaving, enabling the design of preventive measures before the actual decision to change jobs is made. Thus, retention management is transformed from a reaction to an event into a risk management process.

A related area remains the monitoring of engagement levels and organisational health. The use of text analysis methods allows for the processing of anonymous employee opinions, survey results, or internal reports, enabling the identification of trends in morale, work overload, or the quality of cooperation between individuals. This knowledge supports managers in taking corrective action and shaping the work environment in a more informed manner.

The transformation also extends to recruitment processes. Automating the initial selection of candidates allows for the efficient processing of large volumes of applications while maintaining consistent evaluation criteria. Models that match a candidate's competency profile to the requirements of the position increase the transparency of decisions and enable faster identification of individuals with the highest potential. In addition, job advertisement language analytics helps to optimise them in terms of readability, accessibility, and compliance with diversity policy objectives (Guenole & Feinzig, 2018).

An important dimension of AI applications concerns employee development management. Recommendation systems can indicate optimal paths for improving qualifications by combining information about current competence levels, organisational needs, and projected technological and market changes. This enables more precise planning of investments in development, while increasing the internal mobility of employees.

Strategic employment planning is also becoming increasingly important. Predictive models support forecasting future demand for specific competency profiles, taking into account scenarios of growth, automation, and regulatory changes. This allows the organisation to make timely decisions about recruitment, retraining, or relocation of resources, minimising the risk of staff shortages.

These functions are complemented by work performance analytics. AI enables the identification of factors affecting team productivity, the relationship between organisational structure and performance, and the effectiveness of incentive programmes. These analyses support the design of more appropriate management models based on empirical evidence rather than intuition alone (Zinkiewicz, 2024).

The expansion of the role of AI in HR also necessitates the development of appropriate oversight and transparency mechanisms. The use of personal data and decisions with potential consequences for employees' careers require compliance with legal regulations, the reduction of algorithmic bias, and a balance between automation and managerial responsibility.

As a result, the implementation of AI leads to an environment in which personnel decisions are more predictable, consistent and linked to the strategic goals of the organisation. HR becomes a function that integrates data about people with a long-term vision for the company's development, strengthening its ability to build a sustainable competitive advantage.

2.6 AI IN FINANCIAL MANAGEMENT: PRECISION, RISK, AND REGULATORY COMPLIANCE

Financial management is the foundation of an organisation's stability and long-term development. Its implementation requires high analytical precision, effective risk identification, and compliance with a growing number of legal regulations. The modern economic environment, characterised by market volatility, globalisation of capital flows, and increasing complexity of operations, means that traditional reporting tools are proving insufficient. In this context, Integrated AI Systems introduce a new model of finance, in which analysis is continuous, predictive, and directly linked to the company's operational processes.

The role of artificial intelligence goes beyond accounting automation or report generation. These systems are becoming part of the decision-making infrastructure, supporting capital allocation, risk assessment, and interpretation of the future consequences of business activities (Sarioguz & Miser, 2024). The finance function is thus transforming from an area of historical reporting into a strategic partner, providing knowledge about possible scenarios for future developments.

One of the key applications of AI is financial risk management, in particular the identification of irregularities and fraud. Unlike traditional systems based on static rules, machine learning models analyse behaviour patterns in real time, learning the characteristics of typical transactions (Jain et al., 2024). Deviations from the norm are automatically classified as potential threat signals, enabling control procedures to be initiated quickly. This approach increases the effectiveness of detecting fraud, money laundering, and accounting manipulation, while reducing the number of false alarms.

A similar transformation applies to credit risk assessment. Modern analytical models use a wide range of variables describing the financial condition, operational history, and behaviour of entities applying for financing (Vesna, 2021). Thanks to the use of advanced modelling techniques, it is possible to create more individualised assessments of the probability of default, which promotes a more rational allocation of capital and reduces losses resulting from wrong decisions.

Financial planning also remains an important area of change. The use of AI makes it possible to move away from static budgets in favour of continuous forecasting mechanisms. Time series models, including solutions capable of identifying long-term relationships, update revenue, cost and cash flow forecasts as new data becomes available. This approach increases an organisation's ability to respond to changes in the economic situation and enables the ongoing assessment of the effects of operational decisions (Addy et al., 2024).

The integration of financial data with information from other areas of activity is particularly important in this regard. Combining production results, supply chain parameters, and sales indicators with financial models means that forecasts immediately reflect actual changes in the company's operations. Managers thus gain access to a consistent picture of the future economic situation based on current operational data.

The third pillar of artificial intelligence applications is ensuring regulatory compliance. The growing number of regulations and their international nature create significant administrative burdens. Tools using natural language processing enable automatic monitoring of regulatory changes, analysis of their impact on internal procedures, and identification of areas of potential non-compliance (Uzougbo et al., 2024). Automating these activities reduces the risk of financial and reputational sanctions while increasing process transparency.

At the same time, AI streamlines the preparation of financial reports by automatically aggregating, verifying, and harmonising data from multiple source systems. Basing reporting on a uniform data model ensures consistency of information, reduces the number of errors, and facilitates audits. The report creation process becomes faster and more repeatable, while maintaining high formal standards.

As a result, the implementation of artificial intelligence leads to the creation of a financial environment in which decisions are made based on current data, forecasts, and systematic risk assessment. The finance function gains the ability not only to control the past, but above all to actively shape the future of the organisation.

2.7 CASE STUDIES

Empirical observations of the implementation of Integrated AI Systems indicate that their value is primarily revealed in their ability to combine strategic, operational, and financial processes into a single coherent decision-making mechanism. An analysis of implementations in various sectors of the economy allows us to identify repeatable patterns in which the integration of data and analytical models leads to measurable effects in terms of efficiency, risk reduction, and increased profitability. The following examples illustrate how ZSAI architecture enables predictions to be translated into operational actions and then into financial results.

2.7.1 Case A: Integrated Decision-making Platform in the Manufacturing Sector

The model in question refers to a manufacturing company operating in a highly capital-intensive environment that is highly sensitive to technological disruptions. Key issues included high infrastructure maintenance costs resulting from unplanned downtime and significant volatility in raw material prices, which made it difficult to accurately plan margins and purchases.

In response, a common data platform was created, integrating three decision-making levels. At the operational level, predictive models analysed equipment performance parameters in real time, enabling the identification of symptoms of potential failures. This information was then forwarded to the financial module, where it was combined with market forecasts for material prices and logistics costs. At the strategic level, the data fed into the production planning system, allowing schedules to be dynamically adjusted to the current economic situation.

The key result was the linking of technical decisions with their financial consequences. The organisation was able to choose operational activities that minimised the total cost of operation and supported the achievement of long-term profitability goals.

A similar approach is observed in industrial practice at companies such as Siemens, GE Aviation, and Bosch, where data from machine monitoring systems is directly integrated with production planning and economic analysis of contracts. This allows maintenance to be treated as an element of value management rather than solely a technical function.

2.7.2 Case B: Optimisation of Sales Strategy in the E-Commerce Sector

The second case study relates to an e-commerce organisation where the main challenge was the inaccuracy of demand forecasts, leading to both excessive capital tied up in inventory and lost sales. The implemented system integrated predictive models generating forecasts at the level of individual products with modules responsible for logistics and pricing policy management.

Demand forecasts fed into operational processes related to warehouse replenishment and, at the same time, formed the basis for dynamic pricing in such a way as to balance turnover with margin levels. A shared data infrastructure ensured the immediate flow of information between sales, logistics, and finance functions.

Similar solutions are used in market practice, for example at Amazon and Zalando, where forecasting, inventory management, and pricing decisions form a single, integrated system that responds in real time to changes in customer behaviour.

2.7.3 Synergy Mechanism

Both the models presented and the experiences of global companies indicate that the greatest economic effects occur when analytics covers the entire decision-making chain. In financial institutions such as JPMorgan Chase and HSBC, the results of risk detection models are directly linked to decisions on credit limits, collateral policy, and capital management.

The common denominator of these implementations is the elimination of situations where individual departments optimise their own goals at the expense of the organisation as a whole. The integration of data, models, and processes means that operational decisions are immediately assessed in terms of their financial and strategic implications.

Consequently, ZSAI should be seen as an infrastructure that enables the management of enterprise value in a holistic rather than fragmented manner.

2.8 CHALLENGES AND LIMITATIONS IN THE IMPLEMENTATION OF INTEGRATED AI SYSTEMS

The implementation of Integrated AI Systems is a process of profound organisational transformation, encompassing not only technological infrastructure, but also decision-making models, employee competencies, and rules of responsibility for actions taken. The scale and complexity of these changes mean that implementations are accompanied by a wide range of risks that go beyond traditionally understood IT problems. Achieving the expected benefits therefore requires systematic identification of threats and their conscious consideration in the strategic planning process.

A useful tool for organising the analysis is a matrix that classifies risks according to their probability of occurrence and potential impact on the functioning of the enterprise. This approach not only allows for the establishment of a hierarchy of priorities, but also for the adaptation of appropriate control mechanisms to the nature of the threat. In the case of ZSAI, areas where the high complexity of analytical models is combined with the legal and reputational responsibility of the organisation are of particular importance (Figure 2.3).

The most demanding risks are those related to data quality and regulatory compliance. Artificial intelligence models learn from available data sets, which may reflect historical inequalities, measurement errors, or incomplete

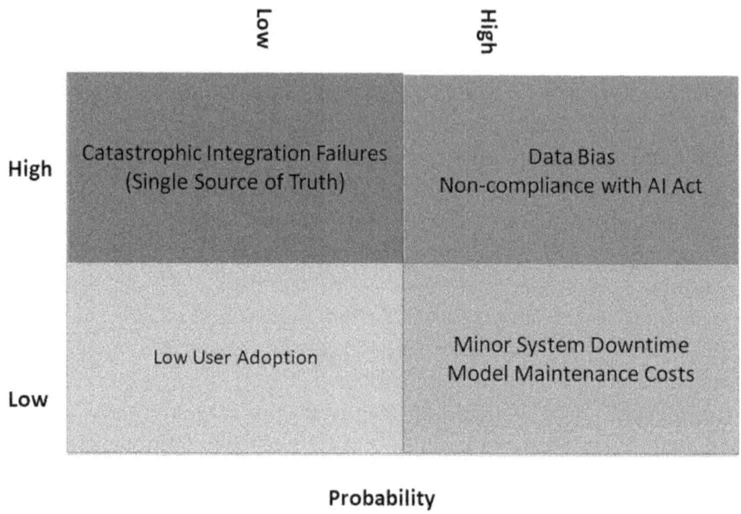

FIGURE 2.3 ZSAI implementation risk matrix.

Source: Own work.

representation of phenomena. As a result, the recommendations generated may perpetuate undesirable patterns, leading to decisions that are contrary to ethical principles, or organisational policy. At the same time, the rapidly evolving legal environment imposes an obligation on companies to ensure the transparency of algorithms, the possibility of auditing them, and control over the way data is processed. Failure to meet these requirements may result in financial sanctions and a loss of stakeholder confidence.

Risks that are less likely to occur but have potentially very serious consequences are of a different nature. In environments based on a common information architecture, data integration is a particularly sensitive issue. Errors in synchronisation mechanisms or semantic definitions can lead to the dissemination of incorrect information throughout the decision-making system. This can result in a loss of credibility of analyses, disruption of planning processes and, in extreme cases, decisions based on false premises. For this reason, it is necessary to maintain extensive validation procedures and business continuity plans.

However, a significant part of the challenges are operational in nature and result from the daily functioning of the systems. This includes, among other things, the need to constantly monitor the performance of models, update them in response to changing market conditions, and manage the technical infrastructure. Although individual incidents rarely lead to serious losses, their accumulation can affect the effectiveness of the organisation, which is why they require structured maintenance procedures and adequate resource protection.

The human factor also remains an important aspect. The implementation of advanced analytical tools changes the way work is performed and the scope of responsibility of individual units. This can lead to concerns about the loss of decision-making autonomy or the need to acquire new skills. Effective communication of transformation goals, training programmes, and the involvement of users in the system design process are key to building acceptance and fully exploiting the potential of the technology.

An analysis of the above challenges indicates that the success of AI implementation depends equally on the quality of technical solutions and the maturity of management mechanisms. Issues such as model transparency, data oversight, and the organisation's ability to respond to unforeseen consequences of automation are of particular importance. As the role of artificial intelligence in decision-making processes grows, risk ceases to be solely an IT problem and becomes part of strategic business management.

2.8.1 Technological, Regulatory and Organisational Conditions for AI Implementation

The implementation of Integrated AI Systems should be seen as a multidimensional transformation project, the success of which depends on the simultaneous fulfilment of a number of infrastructural, legal, and social conditions. These systems interfere with the basic mechanisms of value creation, changing the way knowledge is generated, responsibility is distributed, and decision-making processes are dynamic (Nesterov, 2023). As a result, implementation risks are not only technical, but also economic and institutional.

The first area of challenge remains the organisation's ability to ensure adequate data architecture maturity. The functioning of ZSAI requires a high level of interoperability between systems, standardisation of information definitions and semantic consistency. In practice, this means overcoming the siloed nature of information structures, typical of large enterprises (Collins et al., 2021). Data generated in different departments often differ in terms of classification, update frequency, and reliability. Without standardisation, even the most advanced analytical models generate results of limited cognitive value.

The technological dimension also includes the problem of operational scalability. Models that work well in pilot conditions may prove insufficient when subjected to the full-scale operations of an enterprise. It is necessary to ensure the stability of computing environments, manage model versions, monitor their degradation, and maintain continuity of operation (Kusumba, 2024). These elements require the implementation of engineering practices that go far beyond traditional IT projects.

An important and often underestimated factor is indirect costs. These include the reorganisation of business processes, time spent on model validation, the adaptation of control procedures, and the maintenance of teams responsible for data quality supervision. In many cases, these costs exceed the expenditure on the technology itself, affecting the real return on investment.

Broadening the perspective, one should consider the legal consequences of delegating some decisions to algorithmic systems (Kamiński, 2024). Responsibility for their results does not disappear with automation, but is transformed. Organisations must determine who is responsible for incorrect predictions, what the appeal procedures are, and how the decision-making process is documented. This requires the development of a new corporate governance framework in which the supervision of algorithms becomes an integral part of internal control.

This complexity is compounded in an international environment where companies operate in parallel under multiple regulatory regimes. It is therefore necessary to create mechanisms that enable models to be adapted to different legal, cultural, and market requirements. The lack of such flexibility limits the possibility of global scaling of solutions.

Another category of challenges is the impact of automation on the structure of employment and the division of competences. AI is changing the relationship between expert knowledge and algorithmic analysis. Specialists are increasingly acting as verifiers and interpreters of the results generated by the system, which requires the development of critical assessment skills and an understanding of the limitations of models. This transformation is leading to a redefinition of many professional roles and may cause tensions resulting from uncertainty about the scope of responsibilities.

It is also worth noting that organisations need to build trust in technology both internally and externally. Stakeholders, customers, and business partners expect transparency and predictability in the operation of systems. Lack of public acceptance can limit the use of even the most effective solutions, especially in sensitive areas such as finance or human resource management.

As a result, the implementation of ZSAI requires the development of new leadership skills. Managers must be able to function in an environment where knowledge is generated continuously and often automatically, and where the pace of change exceeds traditional planning cycles. The ability to combine analytical results with strategic intuition is becoming one of the key factors for success.

Ultimately, it can be concluded that implementation barriers are not solely due to technological imperfections. They are the result of a profound transformation in the logic of how organisations operate, which requires the synchronisation of infrastructure, regulations, and work culture. Only by taking all these elements into account simultaneously can the full potential of integrated systems be realised.

2.9 SUMMARY

The analyses conducted in this study lead to the conclusion that Integrated AI Systems represent a new phase in the development of management support tools, in which analytical processes are closely linked to decision-making mechanisms and the operational implementation of activities. Unlike earlier generations of information systems, their function is not limited to data collection and reporting, but includes active participation in shaping organisational choices. The integration of strategic, operational, and financial layers reduces uncertainty, increases the transparency of information flow, and accelerates responses to changes in the environment. As a result, ZSAI become part of the management infrastructure that contributes to the company's ability to build a sustainable competitive advantage.

At the same time, it should be emphasised that the development of this class of solutions is undergoing intensive evolution, and many issues remain open at both the theoretical and application levels. Contemporary research trends indicate a shift in interest from local efficiency issues towards the ability of systems to generate innovation, support organisational resilience, and ensure compliance with social norms. The growing importance of AI in decision-making structures means that questions about its role are no longer limited to technological efficiency, but now also include issues of legitimacy, responsibility, and control.

A particularly promising area for further research is the use of generative artificial intelligence in strategy formulation processes. The ability to create alternative scenarios for market developments, construct hypothetical business models, or identify non standard competitive configurations can significantly expand the repertoire of tools available to decision-makers. At the same time, there is a need to develop methods for assessing the credibility of such constructs and criteria for distinguishing analytical inspiration from speculation devoid of cognitive value. Similar challenges apply to the use of synthetic data in risk simulations, where it is crucial to ensure that models are adequate for real economic conditions.

Another important direction is the development of architectures capable of increasing the resilience of enterprises to disruptions. The volatility of the environment, the increasing frequency of crises and the interconnections between economic systems mean that organisations need solutions that enable them to quickly diagnose situations and reconfigure their activities. In this context, it is crucial to examine the limits of algorithmic autonomy and the relationship between system recommendations and managerial responsibility. The search for a balance between speed of response and control remains one of the central issues for future analysis.

At the same time, the importance of normative reflection is growing. It is becoming increasingly clear that the mere possibility of explaining a decision made by a model is not sufficient if the structure of the system encourages the reproduction of undesirable patterns. This requires a shift in focus towards designing solutions that minimise the risk of discrimination and ensure compliance with applicable legal standards at the design stage. The development of such methods is a prerequisite for maintaining trust in technology and its social acceptance.

It should be noted that the findings presented in this paper are primarily synthetic in nature and are based on an analysis of the literature and observations of economic practice. The lack of systematic research conducted within a single organisation limits the possibility of clearly determining the scale of economic effects and comparing alternative implementation models. The high dynamics of technological change further hinders the construction of stable generalisations, as solutions that are current at the time of analysis may be subject to rapid modification. It is also difficult to assess the long-term consequences of transformation in the area of organisational culture and competences, which emerge gradually and often elude simple quantitative measures.

In light of these limitations, further development of knowledge about ZSAI requires in-depth empirical research and cooperation between representatives of various disciplines. Only by combining managerial, technological, economic, and social perspectives will it be possible to gain a fuller understanding of the mechanisms through which artificial intelligence is transforming contemporary organisations. It can therefore be concluded that AI is not just another IT tool, but part of a broader change in the management paradigm, the ultimate consequences of which will be the subject of analysis for many years to come.

REFERENCES

Addy, W. A., Ajayi-Nifise, A. O., Bello, B. G., Tula, S. T., Odeyemi, O., & Falaiye, T. (2024). Transforming financial planning with AI-driven analysis: A review and application insights. *World Journal of Advanced Engineering Technology and Sciences*, *11*(1), 240–257.

Alhyasat, W., Alhyasat, E., & Khattab, S. A. (2025). Technology trends in strategic management in the AI era: Systematic literature review. *Human Systems Management*, 01672533251322396.

Andrianandrianina Johanesa, T. V., Equeter, L., & Mahmoudi, S. A. (2024). Survey on AI applications for product quality control and predictive maintenance in industry 4.0. *Electronics*, *13*(5), 976.

Batini, C., Cappiello, C., Francalanci, C., & Maurino, A. (2022). Data quality and governance for AI-driven decision making. *Journal of Data and Information Quality*, *14*(2), 1–28. https://doi.org/10.1145/3514220

Bedekar, M. A., Pareek, M., Choudhuri, S. S., Abhishek, P. F., Jhurani, J., & Shah, R. (2024, April). AI in mergers and acquisitions: analyzing the effectiveness of artificial intelligence in due diligence. In: *2024 International Conference on Knowledge Engineering and Communication Systems (ICKECS)* (Vol. 1, pp. 1–5). IEEE.

Bennett, N., & Lemoine, G. J. (2014). What VUCA really means for you. *Harvard Business Review*, *92*(1/2), 27.

Chen, H., Chiang, R. H. L., & Storey, V. C. (2023). Business intelligence and analytics: From big data to big impact. *MIS Quarterly*, *47*(1), 1–35. https://doi.org/10.25300/MISQ/2023/16507

Collins, C., Dennehy, D., Conboy, K., & Mikalef, P. (2021). Artificial intelligence in information systems research: A systematic literature review and research agenda. *International Journal of Information Management*, *60*, 102383.

Davenport, T. H., & Ronanki, R. (2018). Artificial intelligence for the real world. *Harvard Business Review*, *96*(1), 108–116.

Dean, T., Allen, J., & Aloimonos, Y. (1995). *Artificial intelligence: Theory and practice*. Benjamin-Cummings Publishing Co., Inc.

Erraissi, A., & Belangour, A. (2018). Data sources and ingestion big data layers. Meta-modeling of key concepts and features. *International Journal of Engineering & Technology*, *7*(4), 3607–3612.

Eubanks, B. (2025). *Artificial intelligence for HR: Use AI to support and develop a successful workforce*. Kogan Page Publishers.

Guenole, N., & Feinzig, S. (2018). *The business case for AI in HR. With insights and tips on getting started*. IBM Smarter Workforce Institute, IBM Corporation.

Guidotti, R., Monreale, A., Ruggieri, S., Turini, F., Giannotti, F., & Pedreschi, D. (2019). A survey of methods for explaining black box models. *ACM Computing Surveys*, *51*(5), 1–42. https://doi.org/10.1145/3236009

Jain, V., Balakrishnan, A., Beeram, D., Najana, M., & Chintale, P. (2024). Leveraging artificial intelligence for enhancing regulatory compliance in the financial sector. *International Journal of Computer Trends and Technology*, *72*(5), 124–140.

Kamiński, M. (2024). Podmiot kompetencji administracyjnej w zautomatyzowanych procesach stosowania prawa na tle problematyki legitymacji prawno-demokratycznej delegowania kompetencji na systemy sztucznej inteligencji i odpowiedzialności prawnej za ich działania lub zaniechania. *PRAWO i WIĘŹ*, *53*(6).

Keding, C. (2021). Understanding the interplay of artificial intelligence and strategic management: Four decades of research in review. *Management Review Quarterly, 71*(1), 91–134.

Klun, M., & Trkman, P. (2018). Business process management–at the crossroads. *Business Process Management Journal, 24*(3), 786–813.

Korbiel, T., Czerwiński, S., & Kania, J. (2024). Utrzymanie ruchu oraz eksploatacja maszyn w przemyśle 4.0. *Systemy Wspomagania w Inżynierii Produkcji, 13*(2), 26–40.

Kozłowska, J. (2024). Optymalizacja procesów logistycznych w e-commerce za pomocą sztucznej inteligencji i uczenia maszynowego. *Management & Quality, 6*(3), 52.

Kusumba, S. (2024). Accelerating AI and data strategy transformation: Integrating systems, simplifying financial operations integrating company systems to accelerate data flow and facilitate real-time decision-making. *The Eastasouth Journal of Information System and Computer Science, 2*(02), 189–208.

Kusztina, E., Różewski, P., Ciszczyk, M., & Sikora, K. (2007). Struktura ontologii jako narzędzie opisu wiedzy dziedzinowej. *Metody informatyki stosowanej, 2*, 73–88.

McCarthy, J. (2007). What is artificial intelligence.

Min, H. (2010). Artificial intelligence in supply chain management: Theory and applications. *International Journal of Logistics: Research and Applications, 13*(1), 13–39.

Mroczko, F. (2024). Elementy sztucznej inteligencji wykorzystywane w logistyce transportu. *Pedagogika, psychologia, zarządzanie i inżynieria zarządzania–interdyscyplinarność jako oś współczesności*, 9.

Murarka, S., Jain, A., & Singh, L. (2024, December). Advanced techniques in data ingestion and pipelining for scalable big data platforms: A comprehensive review. In: *2024 IEEE 4th International Conference on ICT in Business Industry & Government (ICTBIG)* (pp. 1–6). IEEE.

Nambiar, A., & Mundra, D. (2022). An overview of data warehouse and data lake in modern enterprise data management. *Big Data and Cognitive Computing, 6*(4), 132.

Nesterov, V. (2023). Integration of artificial intelligence technologies in data engineering: Challenges and prospects in the modern information environment. *Вісник Черкаського державного технологічного університету. Технічні науки, 28*(4), 82–90.

Nguyen, T. (2023). Applications of artificial intelligence for demand forecasting. *Operations and Supply Chain Management: An International Journal, 16*(4), 424–434.

Niemiro, W. (2013). Symulacje stochastyczne i metody Monte Carlo. *Matematyka stosowana. Wydział Matematyki, Informatyki i Mechaniki.* Uniwersytet Warszawski.

Olan, F., Arakpogun, E. O., Suklan, J., Nakpodia, F., Damij, N., & Jayawickrama, U. (2022). Artificial intelligence and knowledge sharing: Contributing factors to organizational performance. *Journal of Business Research, 145*, 605–615.

Oleś-Filiks, M. (2025). Sztuczna inteligencja w systemach informatycznych zarządzania w środowisku procesowym.

Pai, R. Y., Shetty, A., Shetty, A. D., Bhandary, R., Shetty, J., Nayak, S., ... & D'souza, K. J. (2022). Integrating artificial intelligence for knowledge management systems–synergy among people and technology: A systematic review of the evidence. *Economic Research-Ekonomska istraživanja*, *35*(1), 7043–7065.

Pisoni, G., Molnár, B., & Tarcsi, Á. (2021). Data science for finance: Best-suited methods and enterprise architectures. *Applied System Innovation*, *4*(3), 69.

Prasad, K. R., Karanam, S. R., Ganesh, D., Liyakat, K. K. S., Talasila, V., & Purushotham, P. (2024). AI in public-private partnership for IT infrastructure development. *The Journal of High Technology Management Research*, *35*(1), 100496.

Prasanth, A., Densy, J. V., Surendran, P., & Bindhya, T. (2023). Role of artificial intelligence and business decision making. *International Journal of Advanced Computer Science and Applications*, *14*(6).

Raisch, S., & Krakowski, S. (2021). Artificial intelligence and management: The automation–augmentation paradox. *Academy of Management Review*, *46*(1), 192–210. https://doi.org/10.5465/amr.2018.0072

Rane, N., Choudhary, S., & Rane, J. (2024). Artificial intelligence and machine learning in business intelligence, finance, and e-commerce: A review. *Finance, and E-commerce: a Review* (May 27, 2024).

Ratajczak, W. (2025). Era sztucznej inteligencji: jak AI kształtuje przyszłość biznesu i gospodarki. *Zarządzanie Innowacyjne w Gospodarce i Biznesie*, *41*(2), 69–80.

Ribeiro, J., Lima, R., Eckhardt, T., & Paiva, S. (2021). Robotic process automation and artificial intelligence in industry 4.0–a literature review. *Procedia Computer Science*, *181*, 51–58.

Rut, J., & Ostafil, M. (2020). Cyfryzacja i automatyzacja procesów zachodzących w przedsiębiorstwach. *Przegląd Nauk Stosowanych, Wydawnictwo Politechniki Opolskiej*, *26*(1), 17–29.

Sarioguz, O., & Miser, E. (2024). Integrating AI in financial risk management: Evaluating the effects of machine learning algorithms on predictive accuracy and regulatory compliance. no. November.

Shakya, A. K., Pillai, G., & Chakrabarty, S. (2023). Reinforcement learning algorithms: A brief survey. *Expert Systems with Applications*, *231*, 120495.

Talaat, M., Tayseer, M., Farahat, M. A., & Song, D. (2024). Artificial intelligence strategies for simulating the integrated energy systems. *Artificial Intelligence Review*, *57*(4), 106.

Thomas, M., Baxter, G. J., & Todd, I. (2016). Normalised model-based processing diagrams for additive layer manufacture of engineering alloys. *Acta Materialia*, *108*, 26–35.

Uzougbo, N. S., Ikegwu, C. G., & Adewusi, A. O. (2024). Legal accountability and ethical considerations of AI in financial services. *GSC Advanced Research and Reviews*, *19*(02), 130–142.

Verma, P. (2024). Transforming supply chains through AI: Demand forecasting, inventory management, and dynamic optimization. *Integrated Journal of Science and Technology*, *1*(3).

Vesna, B. A. (2021). Challenges of financial risk management: AI applications. *Management: Journal of Sustainable Business and Management Solutions in Emerging Economies*, *26*(3), 27–34.

Wiering, M. A., & Van Otterlo, M. (2012). Reinforcement learning. *Adaptation, learning, and optimization*, *12*(3), 729.

Wierzbicki, B., & Zaskórski, P. (2025). Cyber space services and artificial intelligence as determinants of effective operations in modern organizations. *Nowoczesne Systemy Zarządzania*, *20*(3), 63–80.

Zhang, Y., Chang, C., Wang, W., & Xiao, G. (2021, November). An ontology based single source of truth (SSOT) construction approach for aircraft modeling and simulation. In *Asia-Pacific international symposium on aerospace technology* (pp. 81–88). Springer Nature Singapore.

Zhu, J. Y., Tang, B., & Li, V. O. (2019). A five-layer architecture for big data processing and analytics. *International Journal of Big Data Intelligence*, *6*(1), 38–49.

Zinkiewicz, M. (2024). Wpływ automatyzacji opartej na sztucznej inteligencji na efektywność pracy umysłowej.

Zohuri, B., Moghaddam, M., & Mossavar-Rahmani, F. (2022). Business resilience system integrated artificial intelligence system. *International Journal of Theoretical & Computational Physics*, *3*(1), 1–7.

3 Humanoid and Virtual Leaders as a New Model of Decision-Making in Enterprises

Case Studies of Mika and Tang Yu

3.1 INTRODUCTION

The widespread use of artificial intelligence (AI) in organisational structures has fundamentally modified the nature of decision-making in contemporary enterprises. Initially adopted as a support tool for data analysis and automation, AI is increasingly used within strategic, operational, and managerial processes. It reflects a development from *AI-supported decision-making* to *AI-driven decision-making*, in which algorithmic systems actively shape organisational actions and outcomes (Russell & Norvig, 2021).

A particularly significant manifestation is the appearance of humanoid and virtual leaders, AI-based agents assigned roles traditionally reserved for

DOI:10.1201/9781042024131-4

human executives (Skubis & Wodarski, 2023). These entities are not merely analytical systems operating in the background; rather, they are explicitly framed as decision-makers, communicators, and strategic actors within organisations. This development challenges established assumptions about leadership, responsibility, and human agency, and raises questions about whether AI represents an incremental innovation or a fundamental change in organisational governance (Skubis, 2025a; Floridi et al., 2018).

This chapter examines humanoid and virtual leadership through two prominent cases: the humanoid robot Mika, appointed as CEO of Dictador, and Tang Yu, a virtual CEO at NetDragon Websoft. By analysing their decision-making processes, the chapter analyses how AI changes managerial logic, management, project management, and strategic oversight, while also addressing ethical and organisational challenges associated with AI-led leadership.

3.2 THEORETICAL BACKGROUND: AI-DRIVEN DECISION-MAKING AND EMBODIED LEADERSHIP

3.2.1 AI in Organisational Decision-Making

Decision-making has long been recognised as a core managerial function, traditionally grounded in human judgment, experience, and bounded rationality (Simon, 1955). Advances in machine learning, big data analytics, and predictive modeling have significantly expanded the capacity of organisations to process complex information in real time. AI systems are now capable of identifying patterns, forecasting trends, and optimising resource allocation with a speed and scale unattainable for human decision-makers alone (Brynjolfsson & McAfee, 2017).

In this context, AI contributes to decision-making in three primary ways: descriptive analytics (understanding what has happened), predictive analytics (forecasting future outcomes), and prescriptive analytics (recommending or executing actions; Conn et al., 2024). As AI systems increasingly move towards prescriptive and autonomous functions, they begin to assume a quasi-managerial role within organisations.

From a management perspective, the expansion of AI also brings new organisational responsibilities, particularly regarding the control of automated decisions, system security, and accountability. The adoption of AI-based robots and applications requires internal governance frameworks that can balance efficiency, innovation, and human oversight. Therefore, the challenge is not only technological, but also strategic and ethical (Skubis, 2024a).

3.2.2 Humanoid and Virtual Leaders as Embodied AI

The concept of *embodied AI* refers to artificial agents that possess a physical or representational presence, enabling interaction with humans in social and organisational contexts. Humanoid robots and virtual avatars exemplify this approach by combining analytical capabilities with communicative and symbolic functions (Akerkar, 2026; Fung et al., 2025).

Unlike disembodied decision-support systems, humanoid and virtual leaders are deliberately personified. This embodiment facilitates acceptance, visibility, and legitimacy within organisations, but also amplifies ethical and governance concerns. By presenting AI as a "leader," organisations implicitly attribute authority, agency, and responsibility to non-human systems, blurring traditional boundaries between human and machine decision-making (Floridi et al., 2018).

Virtual AI entities enable organisations to maintain a high degree of control over organisational communication and operational behaviour, reducing risks associated with human error or unpredictable individual decisions that may damage organisational reputation or strategic coherence. Their "always-available" and consistently curated presence supports continuous alignment with corporate objectives. At the same time, this controllability raises governance concerns, particularly regarding transparency, accountability, and stakeholder trust (Skubis & Mosek, 2025).

3.2.3 Human Oversight and Accountability

Despite the increasing sophistication of AI systems, their operational legitimacy and ethical alignment remain contingent upon human oversight, explainability, and accountability frameworks. As articulated by Jobin et al. (2019), ensuring that AI systems adhere to human-centric ethical standards requires transparent governance structures that clearly delineate human responsibility in algorithmic processes. This principle is reflected in global regulatory frameworks such as the EU AI Act, which mandates human oversight mechanisms, particularly in high-risk decision-making domains (Ottun & Flores, 2025; Skubis, 2024b).

However, human oversight remains crucial in both scenarios. It ensures that these robotic CEOs align with their respective companies' goals, values, and overall strategies. This oversight also allows for human intervention in unexpected situations or challenges that the robots might not be programmed to handle (Skubis, 2025b).

The human-in-the-loop (HITL) approach is a foundational model for maintaining accountability and ethical control in AI operations. In management and decision-support systems, HITL ensures human judgment at key stages of data processing, model validation, and decision approval (Onat, 2025). However, as Holzinger et al. (2025) caution, effective oversight depends not only on human presence but also on explainability: the system's capacity to render its reasoning comprehensible and actionable to human supervisors. Without explainability, oversight risks becoming merely symbolic.

Emerging scholarship has introduced nuanced models such as human-in-the-loop and human-on-the-loop, emphasising scalable monitoring and strategic intervention rather than continuous control (Cheruvu, 2026; Singh & Szajnfarber, 2025). These frameworks recognise that in complex, data-intensive contexts, complete human supervision may be impractical, yet structured accountability through audit trails, model interpretability, and escalation protocols remains essential. As Sadovski et al. (2025) argue, oversight must be context-sensitive, balancing autonomy and human intervention according to system risk levels and societal impact.

From an organisational ethics standpoint, accountability extends beyond compliance; it encompasses moral responsibility for the outcomes of AI-assisted decisions. According to Vance et al. (2025), the expansion of AI autonomy within corporations risks diffusing individual responsibility unless governance systems explicitly define decision ownership and liability. Similarly, Mohammed (2025) emphasises the importance of bias-resistant and transparent data governance models to sustain human accountability in algorithmic analytics.

In practice, human oversight frameworks function most effectively when embedded within organisational governance structures that promote reflexive accountability, mechanisms enabling continuous human learning and ethical recalibration in light of AI outcomes (McKay, 2024). As AI systems assume greater decision-making autonomy, the future of responsible governance will depend not only on regulatory mandates but on cultivating organisational cultures of ethical vigilance, where oversight is both procedural and principled (Kandikatla & Radeljic, 2025).

Although humanoid robots can significantly enhance managerial processes through speed, consistency, and analytical accuracy, they still face limitations in emotional intelligence and interpersonal leadership skills. These deficits may affect trust-building, motivation, and team cohesion, which remain crucial for effective project execution. Therefore, humanoid robot leadership is most effective when integrated into a hybrid model, combining AI efficiency with human empathy and ethical judgment (Skubis, 2025c).

3.3 METHODOLOGY: CASE STUDY APPROACH

This chapter adopts a qualitative case study methodology to examine AI-based leadership in practice. Case studies are particularly suitable for exploring emerging phenomena where empirical data remain limited and contextual understanding is essential (Yin, 2018). This methodological approach is appropriate for enterprise-management research because it enables a structured examination of decision-making architectures, governance mechanisms, and strategic narratives at the organisational level. Since humanoid and virtual CEO cases remain rare and highly contextual, an exploratory case-based design allows for theory-informed interpretation while recognising the limitations of public data availability.

3.3.1 Case Selection

The cases of Mika and Tang Yu were selected due to their prominence, contrasting forms of embodiment (humanoid vs. virtual), and availability of publicly documented organisational narratives. Together, they demonstrate changes in AI leadership across different cultural and industrial contexts.

The humanoid CEO Mika is associated with the company Dictador, while the virtual CEO Tang Yu operates within NetDragon Websoft. The cases represent two distinct organisational environments: a premium consumer goods brand and a high-velocity technology and gaming enterprise. This contrast supports comparative interpretation of AI leadership across sectors characterised by different decision tempos, data structures, and market dynamics.

The case selection follows theoretical sampling logic, focusing on:

- visibility of AI in executive decision-making roles,
- organisational framing of AI as leadership rather than support tool,
- availability of multi-source public documentation,
- cross-cultural and cross-industry contrast.

3.3.2 Data Sources

The analysis is based on corporate press releases and official statements, executive interviews published in business and technology media, publicly available corporate reports, secondary academic literature on AI, leadership, and decision-making.

A limitation of this approach is that detailed technical specifications of both systems are proprietary and not publicly disclosed. Therefore, the chapter focuses on decision-making functions as described by organisations and observable outcomes, rather than on internal model architecture. To mitigate this limitation, the study applies data triangulation, comparing:

- corporate narratives,
- independent media coverage,
- academic frameworks on AI decision-support and algorithmic governance.

This triangulation strengthens interpretive validity and reduces dependence on single-source organisational self-representation.

3.3.3 Analytical Procedure

The analysis follows a structured qualitative content analysis combined with theory-driven interpretation. The analytical process begins with the collection and systematic mapping of publicly available materials describing AI leadership roles, organisational decision processes, and governance narratives. These materials form the empirical basis for examining how AI-based leadership is framed, implemented, and operationalised within organisational contexts.

The collected data were then analysed through thematic coding using theory-informed categories derived from algorithmic management literature, enterprise governance theory, AI ethics and governance frameworks, and decision-making theory, including the concept of bounded rationality. This theoretical grounding enables the interpretation of organisational narratives in relation to established knowledge on AI-driven decision-making and managerial control structures.

Following coding, a cross-case comparison was conducted to identify similarities and differences between cases in terms of decision authority structures, mechanisms of human oversight, organisational framing of AI agency, and enterprise performance narratives. This comparative logic allows patterns to be identified across cases while preserving their contextual specificity. Finally, findings were interpreted through enterprise-management theories and AI governance frameworks in order to support analytical generalisation and to position the cases within broader discussions on AI-agent leadership and organisational transformation.

3.3.4. Analytical Dimensions

The cases are analysed with respect to:

- scope of decision-making autonomy,
- types of data used,
- speed and continuity of decision processes,
- mechanisms of human oversight,
- organisational and ethical implications.

Additionally, the analysis highlights enterprise-management implications in terms of decision rights allocation, managerial control systems, strategic alignment, and project portfolio governance. These dimensions allow the cases to be interpreted not only as technological demonstrations but as organisational innovations that reshape how decisions are structured, validated, and implemented.

3.3.5 Validity, Reliability, and Research Rigour

Methodological rigour is addressed through the use of multiple data sources and the alignment of empirical observations with established theoretical frameworks, supporting construct validity. Internal validity is strengthened through pattern matching between theoretical expectations and case observations, as well as through cross-case comparison to identify recurring organisational and governance mechanisms. External validity is addressed through analytical generalisation to AI-agent leadership theory rather than population-level inference. Reliability is supported through transparent documentation of data sources and analytical categories, as well as the use of replicable coding logic based on theory-driven analytical dimensions.

3.3.6 Ethical and Epistemological Considerations

The study acknowledges the ethical and epistemological challenges associated with researching AI systems through organisational narratives. Corporate representations of AI leadership may emphasise efficiency, objectivity, and innovation while underreporting limitations, biases, or governance risks. Therefore, the analysis critically evaluates claims related to algorithmic objectivity, bias reduction through automation, and performance improvements attributed to AI leadership.

The research also aligns with human-centric AI principles by emphasising the importance of human accountability, transparency of decision pathways, and explainability in AI-driven governance structures. These elements are considered essential for ensuring that AI-based decision-making remains ethically controllable and organisationally accountable.

3.4 RESEARCH OUTCOMES

This section presents the main outcomes derived from the comparative case analysis of AI-based leadership in enterprise contexts. The results are structured around the key analytical dimensions introduced in the methodology and focus on how AI-agent leadership influences organisational decision-making, managerial roles, governance requirements, and enterprise performance narratives. The following subsections summarise the empirical observations and theoretical interpretation, highlighting both the operational advantages and governance challenges associated with the appearance and development of humanoid and virtual AI leaders in executive functions.

3.4.1 Decision-Making Processes of Mika and Tang Yu

Mika's appointment at Dictador highlights an emphasis on operational efficiency in areas such as supply chain management, financial forecasting, and customer engagement. Available data from press releases and interviews with Dictador's management suggest that Mika used predictive analytics to forecast market demand for luxury beverages, potentially reducing inventory costs and minimising waste. While many of the online sources and online press discuss Mika's AI-driven role, direct references to "predictive analytics" may be phrased differently – such as "AI-based forecasting," "data-driven information," or "strategic data analysis". The overarching theme is that Mika's primary function involves collecting and interpreting market data to inform decisions about production, inventory, and market positioning, which aligns with the concept of predictive analytics for demand forecasting and inventory optimisation.

From the viewpoint of enterprise decision-making, this reflects a change towards algorithmic operational control, where forecasting and optimisation become embedded in executive routines. In organisations operating under cost pressure and competitive dynamics, demand prediction and inventory efficiency are critical drivers of profitability and sustainability. Therefore, Mika's role can be interpreted as an attempt to integrate AI-driven operational intelligence into the leadership layer of the enterprise.

Mika's core function centres on continuous data analysis and information synthesis, which directly informs how she makes decisions. This process includes collating market intelligence, spotting client prospects, and matching potential creative collaborators – functions that are critical to Dictador's strategic positioning as a premium brand.

Mika's approach to decision-making is characterised by her 24/7 operational capacity, enabling round-the-clock data scanning. Unlike human executives who adhere to conventional work schedules, she can immediately detect and respond to shifts in market trends or consumer preferences. For instance, when deciding on potential design partnerships for Dictador's bottle collections, Mika reportedly draws on an extensive database of artist portfolios, social media engagement metrics, and consumer sentiment indicators, forming recommendations that align with Dictador's brand identity and projected growth areas.

Additionally, her reliance on automated algorithms aims to preserve objectivity in the decision-making process. Public statements from Dictador frequently highlight the notion that Mika's data-driven assessments avoid the subjectivity or unintentional favouritism that can colour human judgment. By assessing numeric signals, such as client purchasing histories or brand compatibility scores, Mika can compile lists of recommended actions that are purportedly free from the biases introduced by personal relationships or intuitive hunches.

In enterprise management terms, this organisational framing positions Mika as a mechanism for standardisation and rationalisation of executive decision-making. However, "objectivity" in algorithmic decision-making is not guaranteed, as it depends on the data used for training and evaluation. Therefore, while companies may promote AI leadership as bias-free, enterprise governance requires continuous auditing and monitoring of decision quality, fairness, and unintended discriminatory outcomes.

Importantly, Mika's role extends to overseeing the projects, a decentralised autonomous organisation affiliated with the company. In this context, her decision-making involves assessing community input and project proposals, then identifying which endeavours show the most promise based on established performance metrics or strategic objectives. While specific technical details of her algorithms remain proprietary, her ability to automate real-time data collection and filtering is designed to create more agile and informed decision pathways.

Similarly, Tang Yu, operating as a virtual CEO at NetDragon Websoft, synthesises large data sets derived from user gaming behaviour, revenue models, and resource allocation metrics. Tang Yu's capacity to operate around the clock allows it to continuously gather, synthesise, and assess large data sets: from user gaming behaviour to revenue and resource allocation metrics. This persistent analytics loop means potential issues or emerging trends can be identified earlier than they might be by human teams working standard hours.

Given its 24/7 analytical function, Tang Yu can accelerate the decision-making cycle by quickly spotting inefficiencies or opportunities. According to NetDragon's public statements, this quicker response time leads to faster iterations in developing new product features and potentially reduces delays that might otherwise arise from manual data consolidation and analysis.

Tang Yu also integrates risk assessment mechanisms into its decision-making. By continuously monitoring user trends and operational indicators, it can flag resource-intensive projects that show signs of underperformance or market misalignment. In doing so, Tang Yu effectively closes the feedback loop between analytics and action: adjustments – like reassigning budgets or halting a poorly performing initiative, can occur more swiftly, contributing to a more dynamic project environment.

For enterprise management, the combination of continuous monitoring and rapid reallocation resembles an AI-enabled form of dynamic portfolio management. In fast-moving technology markets, the ability to identify underperformance early and redirect resources quickly is a competitive capability. However, it also raises questions about decision thresholds (what triggers stopping a project), escalation pathways, and ensuring that short-term performance signals do not undermine long-term innovation investments.

While the system's exact algorithms remain undisclosed, NetDragon frames Tang Yu's role as not only driving short-term project execution but also shaping organisational strategy, including talent development. Because AI can analyse performance metrics over time, it may highlight skill gaps, propose targeted trainings, or optimise team structures. This strategic oversight indicates that Tang Yu's decision-making extends beyond day-to-day operational matters, integrating a longer-term perspective on human capital and resource planning.

A tangible result of Tang Yu's decision-making approach is the reported increase of NetDragon's value – up to 10% on the Hong Kong stock market within six months of the virtual CEO's appointment. While stock performance can be influenced by multiple factors, the improvement suggests that investors and stakeholders perceive Tang Yu's data-driven leadership as beneficial for profitability and growth. This reaction underscores a broader acceptance of AI-based decision-making in high-level management roles.

From an enterprise-management perspective, the market response can be interpreted as an external performance-related signal. Investor reactions may indicate not only confidence in operational improvement but also the perceived innovation capacity of the firm. At the same time, it is methodologically important to avoid attributing stock growth solely to AI leadership without controlled analysis, since external market forces, industry performance, and organisational strategy may contribute significantly. Therefore, this case is best interpreted as a strong indicator of perceived value rather than direct causal proof of AI-driven financial performance.

3.4.2 Advantages and Challenges of Humanoid Robots' CEOs in Management and Project Management

Humanoid robots in leadership positions excel in processing vast amounts of data, identifying patterns, and making decisions based on objective metrics. Their reliance on machine learning algorithms and real-time analytics allows them to optimise resources, forecast risks, and propose strategies with unparalleled speed and precision. Unlike human leaders, they are not constrained by fatigue, emotions, or cognitive biases, which can often skew judgment or delay decision-making. In project management, this consistency and analytical rigour are particularly valuable in high-stakes scenarios where efficiency and accuracy are paramount. Robots can act as neutral mediators in team conflicts, ensuring unbiased allocation of resources and promoting equitable treatment among employees.

Despite these advantages, the introduction of humanoid robots in leadership roles also brings to light their limitations. Leadership is not solely about data analysis and decision-making; it involves inspiring and motivating teams, understanding emotional and interpersonal dynamics, and building trust through empathy. Humanoid robots, even with advanced language models and natural language processing capabilities, lack the depth of emotional intelligence needed to navigate complex human relationships. This gap can lead to a lack of genuine connection between the robot and team members, potentially impacting morale and long-term team cohesion. Employees may feel hesitant to trust a non-human leader, particularly in situations where personal or ethical considerations require nuanced judgment.

Moreover, humanoid robots are not immune to errors or biases, despite their objective appearance. The algorithms driving their decisions are shaped by the data they are trained on, which may include historical biases or incomplete datasets. For instance, a robot tasked with project resource allocation might inadvertently prioritise certain tasks or personnel based on skewed data, leading to perceptions of unfairness. Addressing these issues requires regular audits of the underlying AI systems and robust mechanisms for human oversight to ensure ethical and transparent decision-making.

The ethical dimensions of humanoid robots as leaders extend beyond algorithmic fairness. Questions of accountability and responsibility loom large when robots make decisions that affect projects, teams, or stakeholders. If a robot's decision leads to project failure or ethical misconduct, it is unclear who bears the ultimate responsibility: the robot's developers, the organisation deploying it, or the human managers overseeing its actions. Establishing clear lines of accountability is critical to addressing these concerns, ensuring that robots function as tools to augment human capabilities rather than as autonomous entities free from oversight.

In the context of project management, humanoid robots must also navigate the complexities of team dynamics. Effective communication is a cornerstone of successful project execution, yet robots may struggle to adapt their interaction style to the diverse preferences and cultural nuances of human teams. Their responses, while logical, may lack the flexibility and empathy required to address sensitive issues or foster a sense of belonging among team members. This limitation underscores the importance of maintaining a hybrid model where robots handle data-intensive tasks and provide analytical insights while humans retain responsibility for interpersonal and strategic aspects of leadership.

Despite these challenges, the integration of humanoid robots as leaders offers unique opportunities to rethink traditional notions of leadership and project management. By automating repetitive tasks and streamlining decision-making processes, robots can free human leaders to focus on creativity, innovation, and vision-building. Their ability to operate continuously and provide unbiased input can also foster a more objective and efficient work environment, provided that safeguards are in place to address potential risks.

The ethical framework guiding the deployment of humanoid robots in leadership roles must prioritise human oversight, transparency, and accountability. Organisations must establish clear protocols for monitoring robot decisions, ensure that algorithms are regularly reviewed for fairness and bias, and maintain open communication with employees about the robot's capabilities and limitations. Such measures can help build trust and acceptance among teams, paving the way for productive human-robot collaboration.

Ultimately, the rise of humanoid robots as leaders reflects the broader integration of artificial intelligence into the fabric of organisational life. While their capabilities can significantly enhance project management processes, their limitations highlight the irreplaceable value of human insight, empathy, and ethical judgment. An approach that combines the complementary strengths of humans and robots can drive innovation and efficiency while ensuring that leadership remains fundamentally human-centric. By carefully navigating the opportunities and challenges posed by humanoid robots, organisations can position themselves at the forefront of a new era in project management.

From an enterprise-management perspective, the above advantages and challenges directly translate into governance requirements. Organisations adopting AI leadership models should define decision rights (what the AI can decide vs. recommend), establish clear escalation protocols for high-impact decisions, and integrate oversight responsibilities into existing management control systems. Additionally, companies should align AI leadership deployment with change management strategies, ensuring employee acceptance, training, and communication about the role of AI systems. Without these organisational safeguards, humanoid and virtual leadership may increase efficiency but weaken trust, accountability, and long-term resilience.

3.4.3 Humanoid and Virtual Leaders as a Manifestation of the Change from "AI-support" to "AI-agent Leadership" Based on Examples of Mika and Tang Yu

The cases of Mika (Dictador) and Tang Yu (NetDragon Websoft) provide empirical illustrations of the organisational shift from AI as a background decision-support tool (AI-support) to AI functioning as an organisational agent (AI-agent) embedded in managerial routines. In AI-support configurations, AI primarily produces forecasts and recommendations, while decision authority remains explicitly human. By contrast, AI-agent configurations are characterised by continuous monitoring, autonomous prioritisation, and accelerated feedback loops, where AI does not merely provide analysis but actively shapes organisational actions and decision cycles. This shift is consistent with management research suggesting that AI changes the structure of organisational decision-making by enabling the quick exploration of large decision spaces, continuous sensing of environmental signals, and faster translation of analytics into action (Shrestha et al., 2019).

In Dictador's case, Mika's leadership is described as data-driven and built around predictive analytics and constant market scanning. Even though the precise technical architecture remains undisclosed, the organisational narrative implies that Mika's role extends beyond producing reports and instead supports near-real-time decision formation around demand forecasting, inventory-related decisions, and strategic market positioning. This indicates movement towards AI-agent behaviour, where decision cycles are increasingly shaped by always-on analytics rather than periodic managerial assessment.

Similarly, Tang Yu's virtual leadership model at NetDragon reflects an even more explicit AI-agent logic. NetDragon's framing emphasises continuous analysis of user behaviour, revenue metrics, and operational performance signals, paired with dynamic responses such as accelerating product iterations and flagging underperforming initiatives. Such a structure resembles AI-enabled, continuous portfolio adjustment, where AI contributes to decision execution and strategic steering rather than remaining a passive analytical tool. In both cases, therefore, the humanoid or virtual executive functions as a visible organisational interface for AI-agent decision-making, making the transition from AI-support to AI-agent not only technological but organisational and managerial.

3.4.4 Redefinition of the Manager's Role and Team Dynamics

The AI-agent orientation implied in both cases necessarily transforms managerial work. Traditional management assumes that humans generate decisions, coordinate tasks, and control performance through hierarchical supervision and periodic reporting. However, when AI systems operate continuously and at scale, the manager's role changes towards configuring decision frameworks, validating AI outputs, and ensuring governance standards rather than manually producing every strategic or operational decision. This organisational transformation is strongly connected to bounded rationality theory: human managers face cognitive and temporal constraints in processing complex information environments (Simon, 1955), whereas AI systems can expand processing capacity and shorten decision cycles.

In the Mika case, her reported ability to synthesise market intelligence and recommend brand-relevant partnerships illustrates a role that partially overlaps with strategic leadership and creative decision-making. Yet the enterprise implication is not that human executives become obsolete, but rather that they increasingly function as decision supervisors and accountability holders, reviewing AI-generated recommendations, validating assumptions, and ensuring consistency with brand strategy and stakeholder expectations. The presence of a humanoid CEO also introduces an additional management layer: Mika's outputs must be interpreted and translated into human communication within the organisation, particularly when recommendations affect teams, partnerships, or reputational strategy.

In NetDragon's case, Tang Yu's continuous monitoring of performance metrics and its capability to propose reallocations influence team structuring and evaluation processes. This pattern resembles the literature on algorithmic management, characterised by AI-driven influences on work allocation, performance evaluation, and coordination through data-centric logic (Kellogg et al., 2020). In such settings, employees and project teams become both data generators (their actions and performance feed analytics) and decision recipients (they are impacted by AI-guided prioritisation). This can reshape organisational dynamics by strengthening performance transparency and operational speed, but it may also create tensions around autonomy and trust, particularly if decision rationales are difficult to interpret or if employees perceive AI-driven decisions as opaque or unfair.

Consequently, these cases suggest that AI-led executive models require enterprise-level change management: organisations must clarify how human leaders interact with AI systems, how teams respond to AI-driven evaluation and allocation, and how decision rationales are communicated internally. Without such organisational adaptation, AI-agent leadership may increase efficiency while undermining employee engagement or trust in managerial processes.

3.4.5 The Tension Between Decision Automation and Responsibility

A central organisational challenge revealed by the cases of Mika and Tang Yu is the structural tension between the automation of decisions and the attribution of responsibility. While AI-agent systems may accelerate decision-making, responsibility cannot be delegated to the AI entity itself. This creates what enterprise governance literature recognises as a potential accountability gap, where decision outcomes are difficult to assign to a clear responsible actor, especially when decisions are influenced by proprietary algorithms, opaque models, or complex data pipelines.

This tension becomes especially visible when AI leadership influences strategic investment, resource allocation, and project prioritisation. In the Tang Yu case, the described capability to flag underperformance and trigger budget adjustments demonstrates a strong AI-agent mechanism: analytics are directly linked to managerial actions. However, decisions such as pausing or deprioritising initiatives involve strategic judgment and long-term risk considerations, including the possibility that short-term metrics may undervalue future innovation. From an enterprise-management perspective, this raises the question of who ultimately carries ownership of strategic trade-offs: the AI system generating signals, or the human leadership validating the decision.

Agency theory provides useful information for analysing this issue. Delegation of decision authority introduces monitoring and accountability challenges even when delegated to human agents (Jensen & Meckling, 1976). In AI-agent leadership models, the delegation becomes more complex because the "agent" is not a moral decision-maker. Therefore, organisations must explicitly define decision rights and accountability structures, such as escalation pathways, approval gates, and audit trails, to ensure that responsibility remains anchored in human governance. This is consistent with broader AI governance scholarship emphasising that ethical and organisational accountability requires not only human presence but also interpretable reasoning and traceability of decision pathways (Jobin et al., 2019).

In Dictador's case, Mika is presented as a means of increasing objectivity in decision-making by reducing human favouritism. Yet enterprise management research warns that algorithmic outputs are only as objective as the data, assumptions, and training structures behind them. If Mika's decision logic relies on biased, incomplete, or non-representative datasets, the system may reproduce unfairness while appearing neutral. Therefore, claims of objectivity must be supported by operational governance: regular audits, fairness monitoring, and documented responsibility for oversight. Without such safeguards, AI-agent leadership risks shifting bias from visible human decision-making to less visible algorithmic decision-making.

Overall, the cases of Mika and Tang Yu illustrate that humanoid and virtual leaders make the AI-support → AI-agent transition organisationally tangible. They amplify enterprise capabilities in speed, analytics, and responsiveness, but simultaneously intensify governance requirements. For firms experimenting with AI-based executive roles, the critical managerial question is not whether AI can generate decisions efficiently, but how responsibility, transparency, and oversight are maintained when decision-making becomes increasingly automated.

Table 3.1 highlights that both Mika and Tang Yu represent emerging enterprise experiments in AI-driven executive decision-making, yet they differ in the strength and organisational framing of AI-agent behaviour. While Mika's role in Dictador is positioned around continuous analytics and strategic decision support in brand-sensitive contexts, Tang Yu's position in NetDragon Websoft reflects a stronger coupling between ongoing performance monitoring and faster managerial action cycles, resembling AI-enabled dynamic portfolio adjustment.

Importantly, the comparison indicates that the AI-support → AI-agent transition directly reshapes managerial roles: human executives increasingly shift from primary decision-makers towards supervision, validation, and governance of AI-generated decisions, while teams adapt to new patterns of data-mediated coordination. Across both cases, the central enterprise challenge

TABLE 3.1 Comparative overview of Mika and Tang Yu as AI-agent leaders in enterprise decision-making

DIMENSION	*MIKA (DICTADOR, HUMANOID CEO)*	*TANG YU (NETDRAGON WEBSOFT, VIRTUAL CEO)*
AI-support → AI-agent transition	AI-agent features emerge through continuous market scanning, data-driven forecasting, and recommendations supporting operational and strategic decisions (e.g., demand prediction, brand positioning). The AI role is framed as executive-level analytics + decision steering rather than only reporting.	Stronger AI-agent orientation through persistent analytics loops, faster iteration cycles, and continuous monitoring of user and performance metrics. The role is framed as analytics closely connected to action (e.g., prioritisation and resource adjustment).
Redefinition of the manager's role and team dynamics	Human managers are pushed toward oversight, validation, and interpretation of AI-generated recommendations, especially in brand-related and partnership decisions. Teams interact with the humanoid leader as a visible "interface," which may shape communication and trust dynamics.	Managers and teams increasingly adapt to algorithmically mediated coordination, where performance and project signals can drive rapid managerial action. Team structures may be influenced by AI-supported monitoring and optimisation logic, reinforcing data-driven evaluation and fast feedback.
Tension: decision automation vs. responsibility	The narrative emphasises objectivity and bias reduction, but enterprise governance still requires human accountability for strategic decisions and fairness controls (risk of hidden bias if training data or metrics are skewed). Responsibility remains with human leadership despite AI-led recommendations.	Automation is emphasised in risk assessment and rapid portfolio adjustments, increasing the pressure to define escalation rules and responsibility ownership. Strategic trade-offs (e.g., stopping projects) highlight the need to keep accountability human-led, even when decisions are AI-triggered.

remains the tension between accelerated decision automation and stable responsibility allocation, demonstrating that organisations must strengthen accountability mechanisms, decision-rights frameworks, and explainability practices to ensure that AI-driven leadership remains operationally effective and ethically controllable.

3.5 CONCLUSIONS

This chapter examined humanoid and virtual leadership as an emerging phenomenon in enterprise decision-making, focusing on the case studies of Mika (Dictador) and Tang Yu (NetDragon Websoft). The analysis confirms that these AI-based leaders represent more than a marketing novelty or technological experiment; rather, they reflect a broader transition in organisations from AI-supported decision-making towards AI-driven and AI-agent decision-making structures, where continuous analytics, automated prioritisation, and accelerated feedback loops increasingly shape managerial action. In this sense, humanoid and virtual executives constitute visible, organisational expressions of algorithmic decision authority, capable of influencing strategic, operational, and project-oriented decision cycles.

The comparative assessment of Mika and Tang Yu highlights that AI-agent leadership is not uniform across firms but depends on the organisational context and sectoral dynamics. Mika's role illustrates AI-driven executive decision support connected to forecasting, inventory optimisation, and market sensing within a premium consumer brand context, while also extending into decentralised project-related evaluation. Tang Yu demonstrates a stronger coupling between continuous monitoring and rapid managerial action, resembling AI-enabled dynamic portfolio adjustment in a high-velocity technology environment. These differences indicate that AI-based executive roles may develop along multiple pathways, ranging from analytics-led strategic steering to more direct forms of decision execution and resource reallocation.

A key managerial implication concerns the transformation of leadership and teamwork. In both cases, the AI-agent orientation reshapes managerial roles by shifting human executives towards decision supervision, governance, and accountability functions, rather than sole decision production. Teams are simultaneously affected through data-mediated evaluation and coordination mechanisms, reinforcing the relevance of algorithmic management frameworks for enterprise leadership research. This organisational restructuring requires explicit change management, as employee trust, acceptance, and communication structures become critical conditions for sustainable AI leadership adoption.

At the same time, the findings emphasise a central governance challenge: the structural tension between increasing decision automation and persistent human responsibility. While AI-agent leadership can improve efficiency, speed, and analytical rigour, accountability for outcomes cannot be delegated to artificial agents. Therefore, enterprise governance must include clearly defined decision rights, escalation mechanisms, auditability, and explainability practices, ensuring that AI-driven leadership remains controllable and ethically aligned. Without such safeguards, organisations may experience efficiency gains at the cost of weakened responsibility allocation, diminished transparency, or reduced stakeholder trust.

This chapter also has limitations. The analysis is based on publicly available corporate communications, press statements, and secondary sources, while technical system architectures remain largely proprietary. Consequently, causal claims about performance outcomes, including market valuation effects, must remain cautious and interpretive rather than definitive. Future research should expand beyond descriptive cases towards multi-case comparative designs, longitudinal evaluation of AI leadership impacts on enterprise performance, and empirical investigation of employee responses, organisational culture shifts, and sector-specific governance requirements. Overall, the case studies of Mika and Tang Yu suggest that humanoid and virtual leadership models represent a meaningful development in the evolution of enterprise decision-making, requiring not only technological capability but also rigorous managerial, ethical, and governance integration.

REFERENCES

Akerkar, R. (2026). Robots with a sense of self: Exploring embodied intelligence. In: *Artificial Intelligence*. Springer. https://doi.org/10.1007/978-3-031-91084-5_11

Brynjolfsson, E., & McAfee, A. (2017). *Machine, platform, crowd: Harnessing our digital future*. W. W. Norton.

Cheruvu, R. (2026). Human-in/on-the-loop design for human controllability. In: Xu, W. (ed) *Handbook of human-centered artificial intelligence*. Springer. https://doi.org/10.1007/978-981-97-8440-0_75-1

Conn Smyth, D., Dennehy, D., Fosso Wamba, S., Scott, M., & Harfouche, A. (2024). Artificial intelligence and prescriptive analytics for supply chain resilience: A systematic literature review and research agenda. *International Journal of Production Research, 62*(23), 8537–8561. https://doi.org/10.1080/00207543.2024.2341415

Floridi, L., Cowls, J., Beltrametti, M., Chatila, R., Chazerand, P., Dignum, V., Luetge, C., Madelin, R., Pagallo, U., Rossi, F., Schäfer, B., Valcke, P., & Vayena, E. (2018). AI4People—An ethical framework for a good AI society: Opportunities, risks, principles, and recommendations. *Minds and Machines*, *28*(4), 689–707. https://doi.org/10.1007/s11023-018-9482-5

Fung, P., Bachrach, Y., Celikyilmaz, A., Chaudhuri, K., Chen, D., Chung, W., Dupoux, E., Jégou, H., Lazaric, A., Majumdar, A., Madotto, A., Meier, F., Metze, F., Moutakanni, T., Pino, J., Terver, B., Tighe, J., & Malik, J. (2025). Embodied AI agents: Modeling the world (arXiv:2506.22355v1). *arXiv*. https://arxiv.org/abs/2506.22355

Holzinger, A., Zatloukal, K., & Müller, H. (2025). Is human oversight to AI systems still possible? *New Biotechnology*, *85*, 59–62. https://doi.org/10.1016/j.nbt.2024.12.003

Jensen, M. C., & Meckling, W. H. (1976). Theory of the firm: Managerial behavior, agency costs and ownership structure. *Journal of Financial Economics*, *3*(4), 305–360. https://doi.org/10.1016/0304-405X(76)90026-X

Jobin, A., Ienca, M., & Vayena, E. (2019). The global landscape of AI ethics guidelines. *Nature Machine Intelligence*, *1*, 389–399.

Kandikatla, L., & Radeljic, B. (2025). AI and human oversight: A risk-based framework for alignment.

Kellogg, K. C., Valentine, M. A., & Christin, A. (2020). Algorithms at work: The new contested terrain of control. *Academy of Management Annals*, *14*(1), 366–410. https://doi.org/10.5465/annals.2018.0174

McKay, M. H. (2024). Realizing the promise of AI governance involving humans-in-the-loop. In: Degen, H., & Ntoa, S. (eds) *HCI international 2024 – late breaking papers. HCII 2024. Lecture notes in computer science*, vol 15382. Springer. https://doi.org/10.1007/978-3-031-76827-9_7

Mohammed, S. S. (2025). Navigating algorithmic accountability and ethical governance in autonomous data analytics systems: Toward transparent, bias-resistant, and human-centric AI frameworks for critical decision-making. *International Journal of Innovative Science and Research Technology*, *10*(10), 1670–1677. https://doi.org/10.38124/ijisrt/25oct919

Oğuz, O. (2025). Human-in-the-Loop AI in management information systems: Balancing automation, accountability, and organizational control. *International Compilation of Research and Studies in Economics and Administrative Sciences.*

Ottun, A. R. O., & Flores, H. (2025). Trustworthy AI in practice: A comprehensive review of human oversight and human-in-the-loop approaches.

Russell, S., & Norvig, P. (2021). *Artificial intelligence: A modern approach* (4th ed.). Pearson Series.

Sadovski, E., Aviv, I., & Hadar, I. (2025). Navigating the human-oversight dilemma in AI-based systems. In: *2025 IEEE 33rd International Requirements Engineering Conference Workshops (REW)* (pp. 454–461). IEEE. https://doi.org/10.1109/REW66121.2025.00069

Shrestha, Y. R., Ben-Menahem, S. M., & von Krogh, G. (2019). Organizational decision-making structures in the age of artificial intelligence. *California Management Review*, *61*(4), 66–83. https://doi.org/10.1177/0008125619862257

Simon, H. A. (1955). A behavioral model of rational choice. *The Quarterly Journal of Economics, 69*(1), 99–118. https://doi.org/10.2307/1884852

Singh, A., & Szajnfarber, Z. (2025). Preposition salad: Placing humans & AI in/on/over/along/under 'the-loop'. *Proceedings of the AAAI Symposium Series*, *5*(1), 107–110. https://doi.org/10.1609/aaaiss.v5i1.35571

Skubis, I. (2025a). AI and leadership in the age of automation: A critical analysis of generation Z's perspectives on humanoid robot leaders. *International Journal of Humanoid Robotics*. https://doi.org/10.1142/S0219843625500069

Skubis, I. (2025b). Exploring the potential and perceptions of social robots in tourism and hospitality: Insights from industry executives and technology evaluation. *International Journal of Social Robotics*. https://doi.org/10.1007/s12369-024-01197-z

Skubis, I. (2025c). Humanoid robots CEOs and leaders in project management: Decision-making, human oversight, team dynamics and ethics. *International Journal of Humanoid Robotics*. https://doi.org/10.1142/S0219843625500082

Skubis, I. (2024a). *Ética, terminología, opiniones y el mercado de SexTech: un análisis multidisciplinario sobre los robots sexuales*. Wydawnictwo Politechniki Śląskiej. ISBN: 978-83-7880-957-9.

Skubis, I. (2024b). The EU guidelines on roboethics and ethics of sex robots. In: Lütge, Ch., Kriebitz, A., Max., R., & Corrigan, C. (eds) *The elgar companion to applied AI ethics* (pp. 397–409). Edward Elgar Publishing.

Skubis, I., & Mosek, M. (2025). Human-like and humanoid virtual influencers (HVIs): Transforming digital marketing and consumer engagement. *Linguistic and Philosophical Investigations*, *24*(1), 170–190

Skubis, I., & Wodarski, K. (2023). Humanoid robots in managerial positions – decision-making process and human oversight. In: *Scientific Papers of Silesian University of Technology*, no. 189 (pp. 573–596). http://dx.doi.org/10.29119/1641-3466.2023.189.36

Vance, E., Thorne, S., & Okeke, A. I. (2025). Balancing autonomy and accountability: Rethinking human oversight in AI-driven corporate decision-making.

Yin, R. K. (2018). *Case study research and applications: Design and Methods* (6th ed.). SAGE.

Market Analysis *Empirical Perspectives on AI-Driven Enterprise Transformation* 4

4.1 INTRODUCTION

The growing significance of artificial intelligence (AI) in contemporary enterprises extends beyond isolated technological applications and contributes to broader transformations affecting organisational structures, management processes, communication systems, and strategic decision-making. Enterprises increasingly operate in environments characterised by dynamic market changes, technological uncertainty, and the growing importance of data-driven management. Under such conditions, artificial intelligence becomes not merely a technological instrument supporting selected organisational functions but an increasingly integrated component of enterprise governance and strategic development.

The transition towards AI-oriented enterprises reflects broader processes of digital transformation reshaping contemporary economies and organisational models. Artificial intelligence enables enterprises to process large volumes of data, automate operational activities, optimise organisational processes, and support managerial decision-making in real time. As discussed in the previous chapters of this volume, AI-driven transformation increasingly affects entrepreneurship, integrated management systems, organisational governance, and leadership structures within contemporary enterprises.

 DOI:10.1201/9781042024131-5

To complement the theoretical and conceptual analyses presented throughout this book, an empirical market analysis was conducted among 192 enterprises operating across various sectors of the economy, including manufacturing, logistics, trade, finance, technology, and service industries. The purpose of the study was to examine the scale of AI implementation within organisations, identify the principal areas of application, and evaluate the impact of intelligent technologies on organisational efficiency, innovation capacity, strategic management, and long-term enterprise development.

4.2 RESEARCH METHODOLOGY AND CHARACTERISTICS OF THE RESEARCH SAMPLE

The research additionally aimed to assess the level of organisational preparedness for operating under conditions of dynamic digital transformation and to identify the principal barriers limiting the implementation and development of AI-based solutions within enterprises. The study included micro, small, medium-sized, and large organisations, enabling a comparative analysis of AI implementation depending on organisational size and business profile.

Within the research sample, the largest group consisted of microenterprises representing 38% of all surveyed organisations. Small enterprises accounted for 28% of the sample, medium sized enterprises represented 20%, while large organisations constituted 14% of the surveyed enterprises. Such a research structure enabled the identification of differences between organisations operating at various stages of digital transformation maturity and provided a broader overview of AI implementation across the contemporary business environment.

A quantitative research method based on a standardised questionnaire survey was employed. The survey was directed towards managers, business owners, and specialists responsible for technological development and digital transformation processes within their organisations. Research questions concerned the level of AI adoption, areas of implementation, perceived economic benefits, investment intensity, organisational preparedness, and the role of artificial intelligence in strengthening enterprise competitiveness. The methodological framework additionally enabled the analysis of managerial perceptions regarding the future strategic importance of AI technologies within organisational development processes.

4.3 AREAS OF AI IMPLEMENTATION IN CONTEMPORARY ENTERPRISES

The findings demonstrate that artificial intelligence is increasingly perceived not merely as a technological innovation but as a strategic component of enterprise transformation. The majority of surveyed organisations emphasised that AI implementation is no longer treated as an experimental technological initiative but rather as a long-term direction of organisational development with direct implications for operational efficiency and competitive advantage.

Respondents highlighted that intelligent systems primarily contribute to accelerating organisational processes, reducing operational costs, improving analytical capabilities, and enhancing the quality and speed of managerial decision-making. Particularly important were solutions based on big data analytics, administrative process automation, predictive systems, and intelligent decision-support infrastructures.

The empirical findings indicate that enterprises most frequently apply AI technologies in areas related to data analytics, digital marketing, customer service, and logistics management. According to the survey results, 68% of enterprises utilised AI for data analysis, 57% implemented AI-supported marketing solutions, 49% used intelligent systems in customer service environments, and 42% applied AI technologies to optimise logistics and operational processes. Organisations increasingly relied on algorithms enabling consumer behaviour analysis, demand forecasting, and the personalisation of products and services.

Respondents additionally emphasised the growing significance of chatbots, intelligent recommendation systems, and automated analytical tools supporting managerial decision-making and organisational coordination. In many cases, AI implementation contributed to improving the effectiveness of marketing activities through more precise adaptation of communication strategies to customer expectations and changing market dynamics.

4.4 AI AND OPERATIONAL EFFICIENCY IN ENTERPRISES

Within manufacturing and logistics sectors, artificial intelligence was primarily utilised to optimise operational processes and monitor organisational efficiency. The findings indicate that 64% of manufacturing enterprises reported reductions in technological downtime resulting from the implementation of predictive algorithms, while 52% of logistics organisations observed improvements in supply chain management efficiency.

Enterprises emphasised that predictive AI systems enabled earlier identification of potential production failures, improved maintenance planning, and reduced operational disruptions. In logistics environments, intelligent systems supported transportation planning, inventory management, route optimisation, and operational forecasting. Organisations implementing AI solutions frequently reported higher levels of operational flexibility and increased capacity to respond rapidly to changing market conditions.

The findings suggest that AI increasingly functions not solely as a supportive technological instrument but as an organisational infrastructure shaping adaptability, resilience, and strategic responsiveness. Enterprises implementing intelligent technologies more frequently reported improvements in operational efficiency and stronger capacities for responding dynamically to external market uncertainty.

4.5 ORGANISATIONAL READINESS AND BARRIERS TO AI IMPLEMENTATION

The study additionally demonstrated that the level of AI implementation remains strongly dependent on organisational resources, technological infrastructure, and digital competencies. The findings revealed that 81% of large enterprises utilised advanced AI tools, whereas within the SME sector this proportion reached only 46%.

Large organisations significantly more frequently invested in advanced analytical systems, machine learning solutions, and automated operational technologies. In contrast, small and medium-sized enterprises tended to implement AI primarily within customer communication and marketing-related activities. SMEs more frequently identified financial limitations, insufficient technological infrastructure, and shortages of qualified specialists as the principal barriers restricting broader implementation of AI solutions.

An important dimension of the study concerned the identification of challenges associated with AI implementation. According to the survey results, 63% of enterprises identified implementation costs as the principal obstacle limiting AI development, while 58% emphasised shortages of specialists possessing competencies related to artificial intelligence and data analytics.

Organisations additionally expressed concerns regarding cybersecurity, privacy protection, transparency of algorithms, and the risk of incorrect or insufficiently explainable decisions generated by autonomous systems. These findings demonstrate that the development of AI-driven enterprises requires not only technological investments but also governance mechanisms, cybersecurity frameworks, ethical standards, and educational initiatives supporting the development of digital competencies and responsible AI management.

4.6 AI, ORGANISATIONAL CULTURE, AND HUMAN COMPETENCIES

The findings additionally indicate that artificial intelligence increasingly influences organisational culture and the structure of work itself. According to the survey results, 62% of enterprises emphasised the necessity of improving employees' digital competencies, while 48% introduced additional training programmes related to AI utilisation.

Respondents noted that successful digital transformation depends not only on technological infrastructure but also on employee openness towards change, interdisciplinary cooperation, and the development of analytical and technological competencies. In enterprises successfully implementing AI solutions, stronger cooperation between technological, analytical, and managerial departments was observed, reflecting the emergence of more integrated and data-oriented organisational environments.

The findings suggest that AI implementation contributes to broader organisational transformations affecting workflows, managerial coordination, communication structures, and organisational learning processes. AI-driven enterprises increasingly require interdisciplinary competencies combining technological understanding, strategic thinking, and analytical capabilities.

4.7 AI, STRATEGIC MANAGEMENT, AND ORGANISATIONAL RESILIENCE

The study also demonstrated that AI implementation increasingly affects strategic management and organisational adaptability. According to the survey findings, 66% of respondents declared that AI contributed to faster strategic decision-making processes, while 54% of organisations reported increased levels of innovation following the implementation of intelligent technologies.

Respondents emphasised that AI systems enabled organisations to respond more effectively to changing market conditions, identify emerging risks, and strengthen long-term organisational resilience. Enterprises utilizing AI-based solutions more frequently reported greater adaptability under conditions of economic uncertainty and enhanced effectiveness in strategic planning and risk management processes.

The findings additionally reveal that enterprises increasingly perceive artificial intelligence as a strategic technology capable of shaping future organisational competitiveness and long-term market positioning. AI-supported systems increasingly influence strategic coordination, resource allocation, forecasting capabilities, and innovation development within enterprises.

4.8 AI AND CUSTOMER RELATIONS

Particularly significant were the findings related to customer relations and communication processes. The study revealed that 71% of enterprises observed improvements in customer service quality following the implementation of intelligent analytical and recommendation systems.

Enterprises emphasised that AI technologies enabled more precise market segmentation, improved understanding of customer expectations, and the creation of increasingly personalised products and services. Respondents additionally highlighted the importance of intelligent customer support systems operating in real time and contributing to higher levels of customer satisfaction and long-term relationship building.

These findings indicate that AI increasingly affects not only operational management but also communication processes, consumer interaction, and relationship-oriented dimensions of enterprise activity.

4.9 ETHICAL GOVERNANCE AND HUMAN OVERSIGHT IN AI-DRIVEN ENTERPRISES

At the same time, the findings demonstrate that the expansion of AI within organisational structures intensifies discussions concerning ethical governance, accountability, and transparency. According to the survey results, 44% of enterprises expressed concerns regarding data security and the transparency of algorithms utilised within decision-making processes.

Respondents emphasised the growing need for clear regulations concerning data usage, organisational responsibility, and the explainability of autonomous systems. Enterprises additionally pointed to the necessity of establishing ethical standards capable of ensuring safe, transparent, and responsible implementation of intelligent technologies within business environments.

The findings strongly correspond with the broader discussions presented throughout this volume concerning integrated AI systems, governance frameworks, human oversight, organisational accountability, and AI-driven leadership structures. The transition towards AI-first enterprises therefore requires not only technological implementation but also responsible governance models capable of balancing innovation, efficiency, and human-centred management principles.

4.10 FUTURE PERSPECTIVES OF AI-FIRST ENTERPRISES

The study further suggests that artificial intelligence will remain one of the most important factors shaping the future development of enterprises and digital economies. According to the survey findings, 69% of organisations planned to increase investments in AI solutions within the next three years, while 57% intended to expand the implementation of intelligent technologies into additional organisational areas.

Enterprises that initiated AI transformation processes earlier more frequently reported improvements in competitiveness, innovation capacity, and operational efficiency. Although organisations at earlier stages of digital transformation continued to express concerns regarding costs and organisational challenges, the majority of respondents agreed that AI development represents an inevitable and strategically important process for the future of contemporary business.

The findings indicate that enterprises are progressively moving beyond fragmented digitalisation towards more integrated AI-oriented organisational ecosystems characterised by predictive analytics, automation, intelligent communication infrastructures, and data-driven decision-making.

4.11 DISCUSSION

The empirical findings presented in this chapter strongly correspond with the broader transformations discussed throughout this volume. The increasing integration of predictive analytics, intelligent automation, AI-supported communication systems, and algorithmic decision-support infrastructures demonstrates that enterprises are progressively evolving towards AI-first organisational models.

The findings additionally confirm that the growing organisational role of AI simultaneously generates new managerial, ethical, and governance-related challenges associated with transparency, accountability, explainability, and human oversight. Contemporary enterprises increasingly operate at the intersection of technological transformation, integrated AI systems, evolving governance frameworks, and AI-supported leadership structures.

In this context, the study provides an important empirical bridge connecting the themes analysed across all chapters of this book. The transition towards AI-first enterprises involves not only technological implementation but also broader transformations affecting organisational culture, managerial coordination, strategic governance, communication systems, and human–AI interaction within contemporary organisations.

4.12 CONCLUSIONS

The conducted market analysis confirms that artificial intelligence is becoming an integral component of enterprise governance, strategic management, and organisational development. Contemporary enterprises increasingly operate within environments based on data processing, automation, predictive analytics, and intelligent decision-support systems, leading to the transformation of traditional management models towards more adaptive, technologically integrated, and AI-driven organisational forms.

The findings demonstrate that AI contributes to improving operational efficiency, accelerating decision-making processes, strengthening organisational resilience, and supporting innovation development. At the same time, the expansion of AI-driven systems generates important challenges associated with governance, transparency, cybersecurity, digital competencies, and human oversight.

The future competitiveness of enterprises will therefore depend not only on technological implementation but also on organisations' capacity to establish responsible governance frameworks capable of integrating artificial intelligence in sustainable, transparent, and human-centred ways.

Conclusions

Human Oversight and Governance in AI-Driven Enterprises

The analyses presented throughout this book demonstrate that artificial intelligence is no longer limited to the role of a technological support mechanism operating at the margins of organisational activity. Instead, AI increasingly functions as an integrated element of enterprise structures, influencing how organisations process information, coordinate activities, formulate strategies, manage operations, and distribute decision-making authority. The transition from AI-support enterprises towards AI-first enterprises reflects a broader transformation in organisational logic, where algorithmic systems become embedded within the core mechanisms of governance and management. As noted by Dignum (2019), the growing organisational role of AI requires enterprises to rethink not only technological infrastructures but also institutional responsibility, ethical governance, and managerial control.

The chapters included in this volume collectively show that AI-driven transformation affects enterprises on multiple interconnected levels. In the context of entrepreneurship and innovation, artificial intelligence accelerates experimentation, enhances market sensing, supports opportunity recognition, and facilitates the creation of new business models based on data ecosystems and intelligent automation. Mayer-Schönberger and Ramge (2018) argue that the growing strategic importance of data fundamentally changes how firms generate value and compete within digital economies. Similarly, Lee (2018) emphasises that organisations capable of integrating AI into core business processes gain substantial advantages in adaptability, scalability, and market responsiveness.

At the strategic, operational, and financial levels, integrated AI systems increasingly function as organisational infrastructures that connect analytical

DOI:10.1201/9781042024131-6

processes with managerial decision-making. The integration of predictive analytics, machine learning, automation, and real-time monitoring enables enterprises to optimise supply chains, improve forecasting accuracy, strengthen financial oversight, and dynamically allocate resources. Such systems allow organisations to move beyond fragmented information environments towards integrated architectures capable of supporting continuous organisational learning and adaptive governance. According to Kellogg et al. (2020), algorithmic systems increasingly reshape organisational control by mediating workflows, performance evaluation, and coordination mechanisms inside enterprises.

The book also demonstrates that AI-driven transformation increasingly extends into the domain traditionally associated with human leadership. The emergence of humanoid and virtual AI-based leaders illustrates a significant shift in organisational decision-making structures. Cases such as Mika and Tang Yu show that enterprises are beginning to experiment with AI-agent models in which algorithmic systems participate directly in executive coordination, operational prioritisation, and strategic analysis. These developments indicate that AI is not merely automating managerial tasks but reshaping the nature of leadership, organisational authority, and governance itself. As Crawford (2021) observes, AI systems increasingly influence social and institutional power structures, making questions of governance and control central to organisational transformation.

At the same time, the findings presented throughout the book clearly indicate that the expansion of AI within enterprises does not eliminate the need for human responsibility and organisational oversight. On the contrary, the growing autonomy and complexity of AI systems intensify the importance of governance frameworks capable of ensuring accountability, transparency, explainability, and ethical alignment. Floridi and Cowls (2019) emphasise that responsible AI governance requires principles such as transparency, explicability, fairness, and accountability to be integrated into organisational and societal systems from the design stage onward. As organisations increasingly rely on AI-driven recommendations and automated decision-making processes, the risk emerges that responsibility may become diffused across opaque technological systems, proprietary algorithms, and distributed organisational structures.

One of the central conclusions of this volume is therefore that human oversight remains indispensable within AI-driven enterprises. Although AI systems may significantly enhance analytical capabilities, accelerate operational processes, and improve decision consistency, they cannot independently guarantee ethical legitimacy, contextual understanding, or strategic responsibility. Human actors remain necessary not only as supervisors of algorithmic systems but also as interpreters of organisational values, societal expectations, and long-term strategic priorities. Dignum (2019) argues that AI should always remain embedded within human-centred governance frameworks where humans retain ultimate responsibility for critical organisational outcomes.

The issue of explainability is particularly important in this context. AI-driven enterprises increasingly depend on complex machine learning and predictive systems whose internal decision pathways may remain difficult to interpret even for organisational stakeholders. Pasquale (2015) describes this phenomenon as the "black box" problem, where algorithmic decisions become operationally influential while remaining inaccessible and difficult to audit. Without sufficient explainability, organisations risk creating governance structures where critical decisions become operationally efficient yet strategically opaque. Explainability therefore becomes not only a technical issue but also a managerial and organisational requirement necessary for maintaining trust, accountability, and institutional legitimacy.

Similarly, the findings highlight that accountability cannot be delegated to artificial systems themselves. AI may influence decisions, generate recommendations, or autonomously execute specific operational functions, but responsibility for organisational outcomes ultimately remains human and institutional. Enterprises must therefore establish clear governance mechanisms defining decision rights, escalation procedures, audit responsibilities, and human intervention protocols. Crawford (2021) emphasises that technological systems always operate within broader political, organisational, and economic structures shaped by human decisions and institutional power relations. Effective AI governance therefore requires organisations to maintain the ability to monitor, challenge, and override algorithmic decisions whenever necessary.

Another important conclusion concerns the organisational and social dimensions of AI transformation. The implementation of AI systems affects managerial roles, employee relations, organisational culture, and internal power structures. Enterprises increasingly operate in hybrid environments where human and algorithmic forms of coordination coexist. This creates both opportunities and tensions. AI may improve efficiency, objectivity, and responsiveness, but excessive reliance on automated systems may also weaken trust, reduce transparency, or create perceptions of depersonalised governance. Kellogg et al. (2020) note that algorithmic management systems can reshape workplace dynamics by increasing surveillance and performance monitoring, thereby influencing employee autonomy and organisational relationships.

The organisational implications of AI-driven transformation additionally extend to changing customer expectations and digitally mediated service environments. Research on transformational customer experience in digital banking environments demonstrates that intelligent technologies increasingly influence how organisations personalise services, structure communication processes, and maintain long-term customer engagement in digital ecosystems. These developments suggest that AI-first enterprises must balance automation and efficiency with relationship-oriented and human-centred approaches to organisational interaction (Skubis & Akahome, 2022).

The analyses presented in this book also indicate that the future development of AI-driven enterprises will depend not only on technological sophistication but equally on institutional maturity and governance capability. Organisations capable of integrating AI responsibly, transparently, and strategically are more likely to achieve long-term resilience and sustainable competitive advantage. By contrast, enterprises adopting AI without adequate governance structures may face ethical failures, operational instability, regulatory risks, or erosion of stakeholder trust. Zuboff (2019) warns that excessive concentration of data and algorithmic control without appropriate safeguards may lead to forms of organisational and societal asymmetry that undermine autonomy and democratic accountability.

The findings also indicate that AI-driven enterprise transformation increasingly intersects with broader debates concerning ethics, innovation governance, and emerging technology markets. Studies on innovation management and ethical governance in technologically intensive industries demonstrate that organisations adopting advanced digital systems require governance frameworks capable of addressing both technological risks and societal expectations simultaneously. These governance challenges become particularly important in environments where AI systems influence organisational behaviour, communication processes, and strategic decision-making structures (Skubis, 2024a; Skubis, 2024b).

Importantly, this volume adopts a perspective that avoids both technological determinism and simplistic optimism regarding artificial intelligence. AI should neither be viewed as an autonomous replacement for human management nor reduced to a neutral technological tool. Instead, AI constitutes a socio-technical system embedded within organisational, economic, ethical, and political contexts. Its consequences depend on how enterprises design governance frameworks, allocate responsibility, shape organisational cultures, and define the relationship between human judgment and algorithmic decision-making. Bostrom (2014) emphasises that the long-term implications of increasingly autonomous AI systems depend fundamentally on the governance structures and strategic choices established by human institutions.

The transition towards AI-first enterprises therefore represents not only a technological transformation but also a profound reconfiguration of organisational governance and managerial logic. Questions concerning who controls AI systems, how decisions are validated, how accountability is maintained, and how ethical standards are enforced become central to the future of enterprise management. Human oversight, explainability, and accountability emerge as critical conditions for ensuring that AI-driven enterprises remain strategically coherent, socially responsible, and organisationally sustainable.

The future development of AI-driven enterprises may also increasingly depend on interdisciplinary approaches combining sustainability, governance, and digital innovation. Research on AI-supported and human-centric management models in smart city environments demonstrates that intelligent systems require governance structures capable of integrating technological advancement with social responsibility, long-term planning, and sustainable organisational coordination. Similar principles are likely to become increasingly relevant within enterprise governance models operating under conditions of advanced AI integration (Skubis et al.,2024).

Ultimately, the findings of this book suggest that the future of enterprises will likely be characterised not by the replacement of human actors by artificial intelligence, but by increasingly complex forms of interaction between human and algorithmic systems. The challenge for contemporary organisations is therefore not simply to implement AI technologies, but to develop governance models capable of integrating artificial intelligence in ways that enhance innovation and efficiency while preserving human responsibility, ethical control, and strategic coherence within organisational life.

REFERENCES

Bostrom, N. (2014). *Superintelligence: Paths, dangers, strategies.* Oxford University Press.

Crawford, K. (2021). *Atlas of AI: Power, politics, and the planetary costs of artificial intelligence.* Yale University Press.

Dignum, V. (2019). *Responsible artificial intelligence: How to develop and use AI in a responsible way.* Springer. https://doi.org/10.1007/978-3-030-30371-6

Floridi, L., & Cowls, J. (2019). A unified framework of five principles for AI in society. *Harvard Data Science Review, 1*(1). https://doi.org/10.1162/99608f92.8cd550d1

Kellogg, K. C., Valentine, M. A., & Christin, A. (2020). Algorithms at work: The new contested terrain of control. *Academy of Management Annals, 14*(1), 366–410. https://doi.org/10.5465/annals.2018.0174

Lee, K.-F. (2018). *AI superpowers: China, Silicon Valley, and the new world order.* Houghton Mifflin Harcourt.

Mayer-Schönberger, V., & Ramge, T. (2018). *Reinventing capitalism in the age of big data.* Basic Books.

Pasquale, F. (2015). *The black box society: The secret algorithms that control money and information.* Harvard University Press.

Skubis, I. (2024a). *Ética, terminología, opiniones y el mercado de SexTech. un análisis multidisciplinario sobre los robots sexuales.* Wydawnictwo Politechniki Śląskiej.

Skubis, I. (2024b). Seksroboty – zarządzanie etyką i zarządzanie innowacjami w branży SexTech. *Management and Quality, 6*(3), 211–232.

Skubis, I., & Akahome, J. (2022). Exploring transformational customer experience in digital banking: An exploratory study. *Organization & Management Scientific Quarterly, 3*, 97–112. https://doi.org/10.29119/1899-6116.2022.59.7

Skubis, I., Wolniak, R., & Grebski, W. (2024). AI and human-centric approach in smart cities management: Case studies from Silesian and Lesser Poland Voivodships. *Sustainability, 16*(18), 8279. https://doi.org/10.3390/su16188279

Zuboff, S. (2019). *The age of surveillance capitalism*: *The fight for a human future at the new frontier of power*. PublicAffairs.

Index

Note: Page references in *italics* indicate figures, and **bold** indicate tables.

For Product Safety Concerns and Information please contact our EU
representative GPSR@taylorandfrancis.com
Taylor & Francis Verlag GmbH, Kaufingerstraße 24, 80331 München, Germany

www.ingramcontent.com/pod-product-compliance
Ingram Content Group UK Ltd.
Pitfield, Milton Keynes, MK11 3LW, UK
UKHW022157190926
475702UK00003B/79

* 9 7 8 1 0 4 1 4 0 7 0 0 3 *